textural SPACE

foreword

Ian Dumelow

In an age when the common medium of exchange is the electronic screen and global communication is a daily reality, TEXTURAL SPACE is a reminder of the immediacy of addressing the work of another culture in the direct and physical context of an exhibition. Standing in the gallery before such large spatial constructions, each finely conceived and executed and handled with such articulacy and precision, is to experience a group of work that is both strongly coherent and diverse, that references its craft traditions whilst freely expressing its own time and place and that stands as a powerful counterpoint to much of contemporary UK. textiles.

TEXTURAL SPACE is the vision of its curator Lesley Millar, and builds upon her earlier exhibition of UK. Textiles, Revelation, which toured Japan in 1998. Its benefit is not simply in bringing to the attention of UK. artists, students and public an unrivalled collection of contemporary Japanese work, but as an ongoing collaboration between artists. The exhibition, related commissioned work and an educational programme, provide opportunities for an exploration of the approaches and attitudes that inform the work and contrast with that of the UK.

It is also a coming together in many other senses, the crossing and re-crossing of paths, each of which lends a further dimension to the exhibition. The Surrey Institute of Art & Design University College in a number of ways is an entirely natural point of origin for TEXTURAL SPACE. The Institute, which currently has many Japanese students attending its programmes, has had long associations with Japan in a variety of capacities and continues to exchange students and build relationships with its peer academic institutions in Japan. This concern to promote knowledge and international understanding through the practical exchange of ideas lies at the heart both of the exhibition and of the Institute's educational mission.

It is also entirely consonant with the aims of Japan 2001, a series of Anglo-Japanese cultural events of which the exhibition is a part, which is intended to highlight and encourage just such interchange.

It is also appropriate because of other long-standing contacts between the Institute and Japan, which acknowledge in both cultures a common respect for craftsmanship and chart its development. In the 1940's, Henry Hammond and Ella Mcleod, themselves notable practitioners and employed by the Institute as the Heads respectively of Ceramics and Weaving, came together with a group of contemporaries to form the Crafts Study Centre. The Centre was driven by a philosophy of handwork that had strong associations with the honesty and integrity of Japanese craft practices. The Centre's unique collection and archive exemplifies this approach through the work of makers such as Bernard Leach, himself profoundly influenced by his Japanese colleagues, Shoji Hamada and Soetsu Yanagi.

The Centre, which was founded originally in Bath, UK., has recently re-located its holdings to the Surrey Institute of Art & Design thereby re-establishing, not only a link with its own academic past and the development of Ceramics and Woven Textiles, but with the philosophical discourse developed between artistic practices in England and Japan.

TEXTURAL SPACE presents an opportunity to test and examine our own response to developments in Japanese textiles which retain a strong central identity to their subject and demonstrate in the work a continuity of concern for particular fundamental values, whilst developing bold new forms of expression. Here is a creative dynamic which binds together artists of different nationalities in a commonly-founded experience and at the same time separates them by their cultural performance. In this respect, and perhaps more importantly, TEXTURAL SPACE may be seen not simply as an outstanding exhibit, but as a further chapter in an evolving dialogue between groups of artists in the two countries.

Ian Dumelow
Dean, Faculty of Design
Surrey Institute of Art & Design University College, UK.

始めに
イアン デュームロウ

■ 電子画面が普通の交換媒体となり グローバルコミュニケーションが日常茶飯事になったこの時代、直接的で物理的な展示では、他の文化に早急に取り組まなければならないと、キスタイル スペース(織物空間)は思い出させてくれます。画廊でこのように巨大で空間のある構築物の前に立つと、それぞれの作品が明確さと精緻さとをもって繊細に描かれ、また、仕上げられて取り扱われているために、多様性がありながら非常に統制のとれた作品群、自由に自分の時間と空間を表現しながらも伝統工芸を活かした作品群を眺めることになります。これらはまた、現代の英国織物の多くとは非常に対照的な作品でもあります。

テキスタイル スペースとは、レズリー ミラー館長のビジョンです。同館長は1998年に日本で英国織物の初期の展示作品「黙示」を展示しましたが、テキスタイルスペースはこの展示作品に基づいています。この展示では、比類なき現代の日本作品へと英国の芸術家、学生、世論の注意を引いただけでなく、今も芸術家の間で協力が続いているという利点がありました。この展示作品は依頼作品でしたが、展示や教育プログラムでは、英国や英国とは対照的な作品のアプローチや、その作品を示す心構えを探求する機会があります。

ここでは、数多くの異なる発想が集まり、道も交差しては離れ、離れてはまた交差し、このすべてにより更に展示の次元が広がっています。芸術&デザイン大学調査研究所は、多くの意味でテキスタイルスペースの自然発祥のすべての源です。現在、数多くの日本人学生が同研究所のプログラムに参加していますが、同研究所と日本との関係は長く、様々な規模の活動をしています。今後も学生の交換留学を実施し続け、日本の学究機関の仲間達との関係を築いていきます。実践的な発想を交換して知識と国際理解を促進しようとすることは、同研究所の教育的使命や展示の双方の根本にある思いなのです。

また、2001年の日本の目的とも完全に一致しています。一連の英日文化行事の一環として展示が組み込まれており、まさにこのような文化の交換を際立たせて奨励するのです。

これはまた、その他にも日本と同研究所の間に長い付き合いがあることからも適切でしょう。長く付きあううちに、双方の文化で工芸が一般的に尊敬されており、また発展しつつあることもわかりました。1940年代には、ヘンリー ハモンドとエラ マクリードが同僚達と共に工芸研究センターを設立しています。この2人自身が著名な専門家であり、それぞれ工芸研究センターの陶器及び織物の責任者となりました。手作り工芸の哲学が当センターの原動力であり、日本の工芸技術の実直さや高潔さと強い関連性があります。同センター独自のコレクションと収集データは、たとえば、バーナード リーチのような製作者の作品を通して、このアプローチを例示していますが、同氏自身が日本の同僚である濱田昇児氏と柳宗悦氏から深遠な影響を受けています。

同センターはもともとは英国のバースで設立されましたが、最近、芸術&デザイン研究所に居を移しました。その学究的な過去を陶芸や織物テキスタイルの開発に組み合わせるだけでなく、日本と英国の芸術の間に発展した哲学的な話にも結びつけています。

テキスタイル スペースは、日本の織物開発への同センターの回答を検証して吟味する良い機会となっています。日本の織物には、強烈な核となるアイデンティティがあり、作品では特定の根本的価値観への思いがいつも表現されています。しかし、その一方で、大胆で新しい表現も生まれてくるのです。ここにダイナミックな創造が見てとれます。これにより、様々な国籍の芸術家達が、その共通経験を基礎にして結び付いています。そして、同時にそれぞれの文化的パフォーマンスにより分けられてもいるのです。

この観点から見ておそらく更に重要なのは、テキスタイルスペースは単に素晴らしい展示なのではなく、2国の芸術家グループ間で対話を進める際の次のステップであるということでしょう。

イアン デュームロウ
デザイン学科長
英国芸術&デザイン大学調査研究所

TEXTURAL SPACE: contemporary Japanese textile art

Lesley Millar

In 1996 I organised an exhibition of artists who use textiles and textile related techniques to explore issues of contemporary concern. This exhibition was called Revelation: textile artists addressing issues and the works investigated ideas about gender, the environment and identity. Revelation toured the UK. and in 1998 was shown at The Museum of Modern Art in Kyoto. Many of the exhibiting artists took the opportunity to accompany the exhibition to Japan and this in turn led to the establishment of a dialogue between UK. and Japanese textile artists during which the differences between the two approaches to their respective work began to emerge. Both Japanese and UK. textile artists base their work on a particular understanding of their chosen materials and the history of textiles. However, as I looked at more and more Japanese work and talked in depth with the artists, it seemed to me that the UK. textile artists, through the use of content in their work, are subverting our preconceptions about the role of textiles as a medium in contemporary art. The Japanese textile artists however, through their textural understanding and sense of space, are challenging our expectations of the material nature of textiles. Again for both, the contextual framework is of primary importance, but for the Japanese the context is the harmony achieved, whereas for the UK. textile artist the context refers to contemporary discourse. These are very basic differences of approach but each has much to offer the other. From these observations and experiences the idea for Textural Space began to materialise.

Since the ending of the Lausanne International Biennale in 1995 there have been few opportunities to see large scale contemporary Japanese textile work in Europe; notable exceptions in the UK. have been Michael Brennand Wood's 1991/92 exhibition 'Restless Shadows' and Rupert Faulkner's exhibition for The Victoria and Albert Museum in 1995 'Japanese Studio Crafts'. Over the last 10 years in the UK. there has been an increasing use of textiles in contemporary art accompanied by public interest and involvement. This is a hard won position for artists working with textiles in this country and quite unlike

the Japanese textile artists are challenging our expectations of the material nature of textiles

「素材空間・現代日本の織物アート」

レズリー・ミラー

日本の織物アーティストたちは、織物を物質としてみる一般概念を覆そうとしているようである。

1996年に、私は、現代生活の中で注目されている論点を織物と織物にかかわる技術を使って追求しようとしているアーティストたちの展覧会を開催した。この展覧会は「リヴェレイション：論点に取り組む織物アーティストたち」と題され、出展作品は、性、環境、個性についての概念を究明しようとするものであった。「リヴェレイション展」は英国各地を回った後、1998年には京都の近代美術館で開催された。出品アーティストの多くが同展覧会の機会を利用して日本を訪問したのであるが、それがきっかけとなって、英国と日本の織物アーティストの間での意見交換が開始され、それぞれの作品制作に対するアプローチの仕方に違いがあることが明らかになっていった。日本と英国の織物アーティストはいずれも気に入った織物生地と織物の歴史についての固有の知識に基づいて作品を作っている。しかし、実際に日本の作品を数多く見て、アーティストたちとの話し合いを重ねるうちに、私には両国のアーティストの間に違いがあることが判ってきた。英国の織物アーティストたちは作品に重要な意味を込めることで、現代芸術の表現媒体としての織物の役割に対する先入観を覆しつつあるように思える一方、日本の織物アーティストたちは、織物に関する知識及び空間に対する感覚を通して、織物を物質としてみる一般概念を覆そうとしているようである。さらに、いずれの国のアーティストの場合もコンテクストが最も重要な枠組となっていることでは共通しているが、日本人アーティストにとってはコンテクストというのは完成された調和である一方、英国の織物アーティストにとってのそれは現代における対話を意味している。 このように両国のアーティストの基本的なアプローチはまったく異なると言えるが、お互いから学ぶことは多くある。「素材空間」の構想が具体化し始めた背景にはこのような観察と体験があったのである。

1995年のローザンヌ国際ビエンナーレ展以降、ヨーロッパで大規模な現代日本の織物作品を目にする機会はほとんどなかった。英国でも1991/92年にマイケル・ブレナンド・ウッドの「落ち着きのない影」、1995年にルパート・フォークナーの「日本の工房工芸」がビクトリア・アルバート美術館で開催されたくらいである。過去十年間を振り返ってみると、英国では現代芸術作品に織物が使用されることが多くなってきており、同時にそれに対する一般大衆の興味と参与も増大してきたが、これは、織物アーティストたちの

Japan where the artists have a secure role in the creative hierarchy. Against this background the confident, authoritative Japanese work will do much to carry forward the debate in the UK.

TEXTURAL SPACE is an exhibition of contemporary Japanese textile art, bringing together 13 of the most exciting and authoritative Japanese textile artists whose works are based in the most traditional craft skills. This inherited and acquired understanding of their chosen medium allows them to create work which may be monumental in scale yet always seeks to establish an essential harmony between its own and its surrounding space.

The artists are working with structure, texture, space, and light to create textile works linking art, design and architecture. These works occupy space, not in terms of mass but more through implication and allusion. If 'architecturally', to define space (to make space distinct) literally meant 'to determine boundaries'[1] then in placing their work within a space these artists are attempting to redefine that space by shifting our focus and blurring the margins. The work is conceived in such a way that it will eventually become integral to the architectural space and not an adjunct to it. Suzanne K. Langer, in describing buildings and sculpture, says that 'the virtual space they create is not pictorial space, but a different mode of spatial apparition.'[2] This can be illustrated by the work in TEXTURAL SPACE which may be understood as absorbing one space to create another.

Those artists with a craft training in Japan and who are working with textiles are creating work which expands the definitions of textile art by crossing hitherto accepted boundaries. Their work is architectonic and it is textile, it is beautifully crafted and it is non-functional, it describes space without enclosing it. The artists in TEXTURAL SPACE are mostly based, or have trained, in Kyoto, a region steeped in the traditional crafts, particularly woven textiles and dyeing, the most famous examples being Nishijin weaving and Yuzen dyeing[3]. Their innovative approach is based upon rigorous training in technical skills and comprehensive knowledge of materials. Order is created through structure with a strong emphasis on the making process and with a very different view of originality and obsolescence from that in the West. In Japan form follows function with the appearance and the meaning of the object accorded an equal importance. The relationship of the artistic process to the artist's self is seen, not as it often is in the West as self-expression, but as a development or construction of the self, and it is that aspirational nature of making which determines the outcome. There is no short-term mastery of skills, the length of time involved is usually a lifetime.

The creative process is intuitive and almost always material-led. When, in the catalogue accompanying the exhibition 'Restless Shadows' Masakazu Kobayashi talks about the potential of string as the starting point for his work, it is that singularity of string which is the determining factor; that is, all that which is discovered to be inherent in 'string'. These artists have a sensitivity to their materials which comes from long association and respect; most have been working with their chosen materials for many years. There is a sense that they don't 'use' their materials but rather work 'with' them, allowing that familiarity to shape the finished piece, directly prompting some forms and prohibiting others. Participating artist Kyoko Kumai has written that 'Materials bear techniques, techniques rouse images and the roused images bear further techniques and materials.'[4] This intuitive way of working is not confined only to textile artists, as basket maker Sekijima Hisako says, 'I try to match the form that the properties of the material suggest with the form that results from my conceptualising.'[5] Always there is the intention that the completed work will work in harmony with its surrounding space.

The relationship these artists create between their work and its contiguous space is one which allows the work to assimilate many aspects of that space including construction, light, materials, perspective and time, so that we, as viewers, become mediating

a sensitivity to their materials which comes from long association and respect

1 Bernard Tschumi. 'Questions of Space, The Architectural Paradox'. Pub. Architectural Association. 1990

2 Suzanne K. Langer Essay No. 3 'Creation' from 'The Problems of Art'. Pub. Scribner's 1957

3 Nishijin – tightly woven tapestry cloth, brocade Jacquard weave, most notably for Obi and Kimono. Yuzen dyeing - freehand or stencil with rice paste or rubber resist. 'Japan Crafts Sourcebook'. Pub. Kodansha International 1996

4 Kyoko Kumai. Introduction to Catalogue for The 6th International Textile Competition '99 – Kyoto. Pub. The Museum of Kyoto

5 Sekijima Hisako. Rupert Faulkner 'Japanese Studio crafts'. Pub. Laurence King Publishing 1995

長い間親しみ、大切にしてきた素材に対する感受性を持っている。

努力の賜物と言える。英国の場合、織物アーティストたちが創造的階級制のなかで安定した役割を持つ日本とはまったく状況が異なるからである。その点で、日本人アーティストによる自信と権威に溢れた作品とのふれあいによって、英国の織物アーティストの今後の発展が大いに期待される。

「素材空間」は、日本の最も伝統的な工芸技術に基づきながらも現代の織物アーティストとしてエキサイティングな作品を作り出している日本人アーティスト十三人の作品を集めた現代日本織物アートの展覧会である。これらのアーティストたちは、芸術表現の媒体としての織物に関する伝統知識を継承し、それに新たな解釈を加えることによって、時には途方もなく大きな作品を生み出したりしながらも、常に作品自体の空間とそれを取り囲む空間との間に本質的な調和を確立することを目指した作品を創作してきた。

アーティストたちは、芸術、デザイン、建物が結び付いた作品を創作するために、構造、織り地、空間、光に配慮しながら作業を行う。これらの作品は空間を占めるが、その空間とは、作品自体が実際に占める空間だけではなく、暗示やほのめかしによって生じる空間をも意味するものである。「建築学的に空間を定義する（空間を認識可能にする）」ことは文字通りに「境界を定めること」[1]であるとすれば、これらのアーティストたちは、任意の空間に作品を配置することによって、観る者の焦点が移動したり、作品と空間との境が不鮮明になるという効果を創り出し、そうすることによって空間を再定義しようとしていると言えよう。その作品は、建築学的な空間と隣り合わせに存在するのではなく、その一部となる。スザンヌ・K・ランガーは、建築物や彫刻の特徴を述べた際に「建築物や彫刻が創る仮想空間は、視覚的空間とは異なる空間的幻影である。」[2]と言った。言わば、ひとつの空間を吸収することによって創造される別の空間であり、これは実際に「素材空間」に展示されている作品を観ればよく理解できるはずである。
日本で技能訓練を受け、織物を専門としているアーティストたちは、これまで認識されてきた境界線を越えることにより、織物芸術の定義を拡大させる作品を生み出している。彼らの作品は、構成的であり、織物であり、それは見事に作成されていて、無機能的であり、空間を取り囲むことなく、空間を表現する。「素材空間」のアーティストたちは主に京都を仕事場としているか、もしくは京都で技能を取得した者たちである。京都は伝統的な工芸、特に織物と染め物がとても盛んな地域であって、その最も有名な例は、西陣織と友禅染[3]である。 彼らの創造力に富むアプローチは、技能取得のための厳しい訓練を受け、素材に関する幅広い知識を身に付けた結果生まれたものである。構造的秩序が確立されており、その中では制作過程が重視されている。独創性と廃退に対する彼らの視点も西洋人のそれとははなはだしく異なっている。日本では、形よりも機能が重視され、物体の外観及び意義は同等に重要視される。しばしば西洋では芸術的なプロセスとアーティスト自身との結び付きは自己表現という形で認められることがあるが、日本の場合は自己の発展・形成とみなされており、如何に向上心を持って制作に従事するかによって良い作品が出きるとされている。従って、短期間で技能に精通するということはなく、通常は一生涯にわたって技能を取得し続けるものとされている。

創作のプロセスは直感的であって、ほとんどいつも素材主導である。展覧会「落ち着きのない影」のカタログの中で、小林正和が自分の作品の出発点としての紐の可能性について話しているが、紐の決定的な要素は、その単一性であるとしている。つまり、「紐」に備わっている特性すべてである。これらのアーティストたちは、長い間親しみ、大切にしてきた素材に対する感受性を持っている。何年もの間、自分たちが気に入った素材を使って作業をしてきたのである。彼らの意識には素材を「使う」というよりはむしろ素材を「工夫する」という気持ちがあるため、完成作品を作り上げることに精通することができ、また、直接的にある形は生かし、他の形は抑制するなどもする。
展覧会に出品しているアーティストの熊井恭子はこう書いた。「素材は技法を生み、技法はイメージを目覚めさせ、そして目覚めたイメージはさらなる技法と素材を生み出すのです。」[4]この直感的な仕事の仕方は単に織物アーティストに限られたものではない。例えば、バスケット制作家の関島寿子がこう言っている。「私は、素材の持つ特質が暗示してくれる形と、私が概念化した結果生まれる形とを一致させようと努めます。」[5]常に、完成作品がそれを取り巻く空間と調和して機能するように意図されている。

アーティストたちが自分の作品とそれに隣接する空間との間に作り上げる関係は、構成、光、素材、遠景、

[1] Bernard Tschumi著「Questions of Space. The architectural Paradox」1990年Architectural Association発行

[2] Suzanne K. Langer著エッセイNo.3 「Creation」。1957年 Scribner's発行の「The Problems of Art」より

[3] 西陣織り：目の詰った綴れ織り。金襴のジャカード織り。主に帯や着物に仕立てられる。友禅染め：糊置防染法の染めで、手染めあるいは刷込み型がある。「Japan crafts Sourcebook」1996年講談社発行

[4] 熊井恭子著「Introduction to Catalogue for the 6th International Textile Competition '99-Kyoto」京都美術館発行

[5] 関島寿子ルパート・フォークナー「Japanese Studio Crafts」1995年Laurence King Publishing発行

influences on the work through the use of our visual and tactile senses. There is a drawing on a particular understanding within the Japanese culture of the differentiation between spaces. Thus the entry room in a Japanese house is a deeply significant space acting as demarcation between exterior and interior, the place where outdoor shoes are normally removed before entering. Once one is inside the space one can understand that the beauty of the space 'depends on a variation of shadows, heavy shadows against light shadows.'[6] It is this relationship between the work, the space it occupies and the space between the work and the viewer which TEXTURAL SPACE seeks to explore.

The artists invite us not merely to be observers of the work but also to enter into and experience it. As we look at the work we don't have the feeling that it is a dislocation of space, asserting its position and making us aware if its 'objectness'. Rather than an imposing of one on the other, there is much more an interactive equivalence or balancing taking place between the work and the space around it. When we see the wrapped paper and cotton work of Naomi Kobayashi and Chika Ohgi's paper works we feel the space is not displaced but rather is drawn into the work. The use of Japanese paper also brings with it other very specific qualities including 'warmth, calm and repose'[7] and as such is very different from Western paper. 'Even the same white could as well be one colour for Western paper and another for (Japanese). Western paper turns away the light, while (Japanese) paper seems to take it in, to envelop it gently, like the soft surface of a first snowfall. It gives off no sound when it is crumpled or folded, it is quiet and pliant to the touch as the leaf of a tree.'[8]

Machiko Agano's hand knitted transparent silk and fishing line and Yoshiko Tanabe's complex netways indicate space rather than enclose it, allowing us to move around, in between, creating a sense of continuum. One of the few UK textile artists in this field is Caroline Broadhead who works with transparent elastic threads. Her current work 'permeates us, we permeate the work. The most recent installation invites us to penetrate the next layer out, the self-defining architectural space.'[9]

There is a fluidity of demarcation within the work, volume is suggested but is not always present. This allows for a variety of ways of apprehending its spatial nature. There is the Japanese concept of 'incompleteness', which is also the beauty of omission. What we in the West may see as 'empty space' for the Japanese is not 'empty' but filled by the creative imagination of the viewer, allowing space for pause, for silence. Within the work there seems to be an absence of the didactic, leaving room for individual contemplation and decisions concerning the experience and evaluation of the work. There is an aspiration toward a condition of appreciation achieved not through a detached view but through the quality of spiritual fulfilment achieved through the work by the viewer.

The architect Louis Kahn spoke of Silence and Light, calling that which does not yet exist, Silence, which is unmeasurable, and that which exists, Light, which is measurable. Between these two is a threshold over which movement takes place and which he called the Treasury of Shadow.[10] The use of light by the artists in this exhibition is as a permeating substance, with the artists drawing with the light, or drawing from the shadow to the light, revealing the forms within the envelope of space. '(W)e first spread a parasol to throw a shadow on the earth and in the pale light of the shadow we put together a house.'[11] Tetsuo Fujimoto's wall hung textiles move from the shadow to the light across the surface. The folds of the work intensify the shadow and also describe the space between the work and the wall. There is also a seeking for the faint reflections of light, 'Collecting little pools here and there,'[12] observing its nuances within darkness, as demonstrated by Shihoko Fukomoto's intense indigo work.

Chiyoko Tanaka, in her use of black, is also using light, not as chiaroscuro but in the luminosity of black, created through the underpinning of the black

the artists invite us not merely to be observers of the work but also to enter into and experience it

6 Junichiro Tanizaki 'In Praise of Shadows'. First pub. 1933/34. Translated and pub. Leete's Island Books 1977

7 Junichiro Tanizaki 'In Praise of Shadows'. First pub. 1933/34. Translated and pub. Leete's Island Books 1977

8 Junichiro Tanizaki 'In Praise of Shadows'. First pub. 1933/34. Translated and pub. Leete's Island Books 1977

9 Pamela Johnson 'Bodyscape: Caroline Broadhead'. Pub. Angel Row Gallery & Northern Gallery for Contemporary Art 1999.

10 John Lobell 'Between Silence and Light. Spirit in the Architecture of Louis I. Kahn'. Pub. Shambhala Publications Inc/Random House 1979

11 Junichiro Tanizaki 'In Praise of Shadows'. First pub. 1933/34. Translated and pub. Leete's Island Books 1977

12 Junichiro Tanizaki 'In Praise of Shadows'. First pub. 1933/34. Translated and pub. Leete's Island Books 1977

> アーティストたちは、私たちに単に作品の観察者となってほしいのではなく、作品の中に入り、作品を体験してほしいのである。

時間といったものを含めて空間が持つたくさんの側面を作品にも持たせることになり、その結果、作品を観る者は、自己の視覚と触覚を使って作品に影響を及ぼす中間的存在となる。 日本文化では空間をいくつかに区別する慣行がある。例えば、日本の家屋にある玄関の間は、外部と内部の間の区画として深い意味を持つ空間であり、屋外から屋内に入る時に靴を脱ぐ場所である。空間の美は「淡い影に対する濃い影という、陰翳の濃淡によって決まる」[6]のであり、それは一旦その空間の中に入ることによって理解できる。「素材空間」が探ろうとしているのは、作品、その作品が占める空間、その作品と見物人との間にある空間それぞれの結び付きである。

アーティストたちは、私たちに単に作品の観察者となってほしいのではなく、作品の中に入り、作品を体験してほしいのである。 私たちが作品を観る時、作品がその存在を主張して「物体性」を強く感じさせることによって空間を混乱させているなどとは感じない。作品とそのまわりの空間について、片方がもう一方を押し退けようとしているというよりは、互いが同等に影響し合い、均衡が取れていると感じる。
小林尚美の包まれた紙と綿の作品や扇千花の紙で作られた作品を観ると、空間が跳ねのかされたのではなく、むしろ作品の中に取り込まれたと感じる。和紙を使うことで、「暖かさ、静けさ、安らぎ」[7]といった非常に独特な特質ももたらすことができる。この点で西洋紙とは非常に異なっている。「同じ白いのでも、西洋紙の白さと、（和紙の）白さとは違う。西洋紙は光をはね返すが、（和紙は）柔らかい初雪の面のように、ふっくらと光線を中へ吸い取る。しわにしても畳んでも音を立てない。それは、木の葉に触れた時のように物静かでしっとりとしている。」[8]

上野真智子の手編みの透明な絹と釣り糸や田辺由子の複雑なネットウェイは空間を包むというよりも、むしろ空間を明確に表しており、あらゆる角度からの観賞を誘い、連続体をも感じさせる。この分野の数少ない英国の織物アーティストの中に弾力性のある透明な糸を使って作品を作るキャロライン・ブロードヘッドがいる。 彼女の最新の作品は「私たちにしみ込み、私たちはその作品にしみ込む。一番最近の展示会では、自己定義的な構成的空間というさらに次の層を通り抜けさせようと試みていた。」[9]

作品の内側にある区画は流動的であり、容量はほのめかされてはいても常に存在するわけではない。 このため、その空間的な特質を様々に解釈することができる。「不完全さ」という日本の概念があるが、それはまた、省略の美でもある。西洋人が「空っぽの空間」と考えるものが日本人には「空っぽ」ではなく、観る者の創造的なイマジネーションで満たされており、休止や静寂のためにあるということがある。作品は教訓的なものを含有してはいないようであり、観る者各自が熟視したり、あるいは作品を体験・評価して結論を出す余裕を与えている。客観的な視線を通してではなく、観る者が作品から得る精神的な満足感を通して得られる鑑賞状況が望まれている。

建築家のルイス・カーンは静寂と光について話したが、未だ存在しないものとしての静寂は、測定できないものであり、そして存在するものとしての光は、測定できるものだとみなした。この二つの間には敷居があって、それを越えてムーブマンが起こるものとし、その敷居をカーンは「影の宝庫」と呼んだ。[10]
この展覧会では、アーティストたちは光を浸透する物質として使っており、光と共に、あるいは影から光へと方向性を持って作業し、空間という包みの中に作品を配置している。「（私たちは）まず日傘を広げ、大地に一廓の日影を落とし、その薄暗い陰翳の中に家造りをする。」[11]藤本哲夫 の壁につるされた織物の表面は、影から光へと移り動く。その作品の折り畳んだ部分は影が濃くなり、そしてまた作品と壁とのあいだの空間を表現する。福本潮子の濃い藍色の作品が示しているように、「あちこちの小さな日溜まりを集め、」[12]暗闇の中に光の微妙な陰影を認めて、微かな光の反射を追求しているものもある。

田中千代子も黒を使う時に光を使っているが、それはキアロスクーロとしてではなく、黒の発光性を使っているのであって、他の色を一緒に使うことで黒を強調しているのである。このような黒に対する深い知識は、伝統的な日本の美学と習慣とに共鳴する。「くすんだ黒と鮮やかな黒があります。輝く黒と光沢がない黒、日光に照らされた黒と影の中の黒。くすんだ黒には青を、光沢がない黒には白を使わなければならない。輝く黒にはゴム糊（膠）を加えなければならない。日光に照らされた黒にはグレイの反射光が必要です。」[13]

[6] 谷崎潤一郎著「In Praise of Shadows」1933/34年初版。1977年Leete's Island Booksが英訳版発行

[7] 同書P10

[8] 同書P10

[9] Pamela Johnson著「Bodyscape: Caroline Broadhead」Angel Row Gallery & Northern Gallery for Contemporary Art発行

[10] John Lobell著「Between Silence and Light. Spirit in the architecture of Louis I. Kahn」1979年Shambhala Publications Inc/Random House発行

[11] 谷崎潤一郎著「In Praise of Shadows」1933/34年初版。1977年Leete's Island Booksが英訳版発行

[12] 同書P14

[13] 北斎John Cage著「Colour and Meaning」1999年Thames & Hudson発行

with another colour. This deep understanding of black resonates with traditional Japanese aesthetics and practice. 'There is a black which is old and a black which is fresh. Lustrous (brilliant) black and matt black, black in sunlight and black in shadow. For the old black one must use an admixture of blue, for the matt black an admixture of white; for the lustrous black gum (colle) must be added. Black in sunlight must have grey reflections.'[13]

Many of the artists incorporate light as an element in each stage of the development and making of the work. For Asako Ishizaki light is not only infiltrating the work but it becomes the strands themselves. Light can be used to illuminate or suffuse, to reflect and reveal both the structure of the work and its relationship with the space, or be absorbed by the surface. It is evident that light conditions play a significant part in the display and understanding of the work, which is not simply 'lit', but incorporates the light as part of its own particular dynamic. The changes in our perception of form and its parameters are conditioned by light. 'Things appear different according to whether they are seen in shadow or in sunlight, in hard or soft light, and according to the angle at which they are seen… Those which are seen in the light of the fire or the moon, and by the rays of the lamp differ by reason of the light in each case;..'[14].

The use of subtlety of light is particularly apparent in certain pieces. For example Koji Takaki's polypropylene works, which do not reflect or illuminate but filter the light through the form in such a way that the eye travels slowly across the nuances of mono-chromatic colour. Whereas Machiko Agano's transparent works, when displayed in natural light, change colour with the differing light throughout the day. Each artist has chosen his/her materials with reference to their light reflecting or absorbing features. Where the light is illuminating, the sub-divisions of spectral colour become more apparent, as in the work of Harumi Isobe, and there is a delight in that radiating light which has many of the qualities of sunlight. Where there is light there is also shadow, the intensity of the light also determines the intensity of the shadow. 'All material in nature, the mountains and the streams and the air and we, are made of Light which has been spent, and this crumpled mass called material casts a shadow, and the shadow belongs to Light.'[15] The contrast between light and shadow defines the space and '(T)he appearance of a shadow testifies to the solidity of an object, for what casts a shadow must be real.'[16] The lit areas are related to the subjective effects of light or its absence; the light is the perception of reality while the shadow is the space for imagination. Shigeo Kubota employs light to create the shadow using the inherent light reflecting qualities of the hemp, ramie and gold thread. In this he is also referring to the traditional use of gold as light in which it 'gleams forth from out of the darkness and reflects the lamplight (retaining) its brilliance indefinitely to light the darkness of the room.'[17] The varying intensities of light are created not by altering the light source but by the effect of the greater brilliance of light through latticed areas in relation to the more diffused light around the form, finding beauty not only 'in the thing itself but in the patterns of shadows, the light and the darkness, that one thing against the other creates.'[18]

Consideration of the movement taken by the eye in exploring the pattern and construction within the work indicates that we are not given a precise focus with a particular trajectory, as in much European art. Here the process of perception is in both the detail and the whole, with the passage from one to the other given momentum through surface texture. If we assume that texture slows down that passage across the surface, then the work of these artists slows down our gaze through a series of subtle, textured intervals. The texture of the work gives us the sense of its surface, enables a visual interplay between our eye and the sensuousity of the surface. In our mind's eye we can imagine how it would be to touch, sensing how it would feel, relating our understanding of the texture to our physical experience. We can allow our memory to guide us towards a re-experience of the sensation. 'The (materials) meaning resides within the realm of each individual's personal experience, as it arises out of a

this deep understanding of black resonates with traditional Japanese aesthetics and practice

13 Hokusai. John Cage, 'Colour and Meaning'. Pub. Thames & Hudson 1999

14 Aristotle 'On Colours'. John Cage 'Colour and Culture'. Pub. Thames and Hudson 1993

15 Louis Kahn. John Lobell 'Between Silence and Light. Spirit in the Architecture of Louis I. Kahn'. Pub. Shambhala Publications Inc/Random House 1979

16 E.H. Gombrich 'Shadows'. Pub. National Gallery Publications London 1995

17 Junichiro Tanizaki 'In Praise of Shadows'. First pub. 1933/34. Translated and pub. Leete's Island Books 1977

18 Junichiro Tanizaki 'In Praise of Shadows'. First pub. 1933/34. Translated and pub. Leete's Island Books 1977

このような黒に対する深い知識は、伝統的な日本の美学と習慣とに共鳴する。

アーティストたちの多くが、作品を練り上げ、作成するという各段階で、光をひとつの要素として組み入れている。石崎朝子にとって、光は単に作品にしみ込んでいくだけではなく、それ自体が構成要素になる。光は、明るくしたり、覆ったり、作品の構造と作品の空間との関わり合いを示し、明らかにするために使われたり、あるいは表面に吸収されたりする。光のコンディションが作品のディスプレイと解釈において重要な役割を果たすことは明白であり、作品はただ「照らされる 」のではなくて、その作品自体が持つ独特な原動力の構成要素として光を組み入れる。形と形の持つ特性に対する我々の概念は光によって変化する。「物はそれが日陰の中で見られるか、日の光の中で見られるか、あるいはぎらぎらした光、柔らかな光の中で見られるか、また見られる角度によっても違って見える… 炎の光、月光、ランプの光に照らされた物は、それぞれ違って見える…」[14]

光の微妙な特性を使っていることが格別はっきりと表れている作品がある。例えば、高木幸司のポリプロピレンの作品は、光を反射したり照らしたりはしないが、光が形を通り抜け、観る者の目は単色の陰影を追ってゆっくりと動くというものである。一方、上野真智子の透明な作品は、自然光の中に置かれると、一日を通して移り変わる光とともに色が変化する。それぞれのアーティストは、光が反射したりまたは吸収したりするという特性を考慮した上で素材を選んでいる。光が明るく光っている時は、磯辺晴海の作品の場合のように、分光色の細分が一層明確になり、日光の特質を多く持った輝く光の中には歓喜が感じられる。光があるところには影があり、光が強烈であるほど影の深さも増す。「自然の中の物質は、山も川も空気も人間も、費やされた光から作られたのであって、物質と呼ばれるこのしわのある塊は影を投じる。そしてその影は光が所有するものである。」[15]光と影のコントラストが空間を規定し、そして「影が現れることで物体の立体性が証明される。なぜなら影を投げかける物は現実に存在するはずだからである。」[16]光を当てられた部分は光の本来的な効果もしくは光の欠如と結び付きを持っている。つまり、光は現実の知覚による認識結果であるが、影はイマジネーションのための空間である。 久保田繁雄は、麻、カラムシ、そしてオウレンが本来持つ光を反射するという特質を使って影を生み出すために光を用いている。彼はまた、金を明かりとして使う伝統的な方法について言及しているが、その場合、金は「灯火の明かりを反射し、その輝きを延々と保ちながら、暗闇の中から輝きを放って部屋の闇を照らす。」[17]光の強さは、光源を変えることによってではなく、照らされる形のまわりの拡散された光に対して、よりきらきらと輝く光を格子を通すことによって加減され、単に「物体自体のみならず、影のパターン、光と闇といった対称が作り上げる効果」[18]にも美を見出している。

作品のパターンや構造を探る時に私たちの目がどのような動きをするかを考えてみると、ヨーロッパ芸術の場合によくあるような特殊な軌道を経て辿り着くべき焦点というものがないことがわかる。 知覚のプロセスは作品の細部にも全体にも広がり、私たちの目は織り地の表面を辿って細部と全体の間を弾みを持って行来する。 織り地の表面を辿る視線の動きが遅くなる時は、作品に微妙な織り地特有の一連の間隔があるからである。作品の織り地を見るとその表面の感覚が分かり、私たちの目と織り地の表面が持つ感覚性との間で視覚的な相互作用が起こる。 心の目で、私たちはそれに触れるとどんなふうであろうかと想像し、どんな感触かを感じ、織り地に関して持っている自己の知識を実際の経験と関連させる。 私たちは記憶に導かれ、そしてついにその感覚を再経験するに至る。「（物質が持つ）意味は、各個人の経験の領域内に存在し、個人とその物質が直接的かつ肉体的に接触することによって生じる。」[19]織り地と人とが出会う時、大抵の場合は目と作品の間にこのような関係が生じるものと思われる。織り地と私たちが再現し直す空間との間には相互浸透がある。 私たちは期待を持って作品の物質的、織り地的存在の中に入り込み、一つの関係を築き上げる。その時にどのような関係が生まれるかは、観る者がどれだけ作品の中に入り込んだと感じることができるかによって決まる。

作品の多くは多層構造を持っている。つまり、ひとつの表面を通して次の表面が見える。これは、織り地の上に織り地を、または表面の上に表面を重ねたり、ひとつの表面をすり減らせて、次にある表面を見せることによって成し遂げられる。織り地は応用過程を経て作られたものと考えてよいのかもしれない。例えば、藤本哲夫は重ねることによってこれを実証しているし、また、田中千代子は浸食でその効果を出している。

14 Arictotle著「On Colours」John Cage著「Colour and Culture」1993年Thames & Hudson発行

15 Louis Kahn. John Lobell著「Between Silence and Light. Spirit in the Architecture of louis I. Khan」1979年Shambhala Publications Inc/Random House発行

16 E.H. Gombrich著「Shadows」1995年National Gallery Publications, London発行

17 谷崎潤一郎著「In Praise of Shadows」1933/34年初版。1977年Leete's Island Booksが英訳版発行

18 同書P30

19 Yasuke Nakahara「Between Man and Matter」1970年にToyojio Hidaが引用。1995年第16回ビエンナーレ展「Giving a New Life to Material」カタログ

direct and physical contact between the individual and the material.'[19] So much of textural experience is based upon this presumed relationship between the eye and the work. There is an inter-penetration between the texture and the space to which we add our re-creative responses. We project our expectations toward the work and, entering into its physical and textural presence, we set up a relationship, the quality of which depends upon our ability to develop fully our sense of complicity with the work.

Much of the work is multi-layered – that is we look through one surface to find another. This is achieved by layering of texture on texture or surface over surface or by the wearing away of one surface to reveal another. We may think of texture as being the result of an applied process, as demonstrated in the intensity of layering in the work of Tetsuo Fujimoto, but texture can also involve an erosion, as embodied in the work of Chiyoko Tanake.

The importance to these artists of nature and natural forms is reflected in both the shapes and textures of the work. 'From the beginning of time nature has been processing all materials and creating textures. Organic life on earth is a chaos of constantly changing textures. Nature has its special, permanent technique in developing these textures.'[20] The Japanese people live in a close relationship with nature, acutely aware of both its destructive and regenerative powers. The artists' expressed objective is to create work which both contains and reflects those elements of nature to which they are most drawn.

There is also a love of natural or 'raw' materials, fibres exposed, structures revealed. 'For instance, in traditional Japanese wooden architecture, the wooden parts are left unvarnished... To Japanese sensibilities an unvarnished surface which has been aged by sun and weather looks warmer and friendlier.'[21] The viewer has the sense that, rather than having become purely the medium for expression, like canvas for a painting, the material has retained and enhanced its identity, yet still has all the essential qualities of cotton or paper or stainless steel. The architect Eisaku Ushida expressed it in this way 'I would pass the rawness of Japanese culture to our children – raw fish and raw material, naked feet in the house, wooden baths – that kind of sensuousness, raw sensitivity.'[22] This approach gives the finished work a residual energy that could be traced to the raw and unrefined origins of the material.

The texture of the surface emphasises the subtle harmony achieved by extending the inherent possibilities of the material, a working with, rather than a subjugation. Within this context of respect for the material, even with that which is most resistant, for example polypropylene, we feel it has arrived in its particular form through wholly sympathetic handling. The different tones, the strongest contrasts combine with the softness, purity, freshness or dryness of harmonious textures, all indicating the familiarity and understanding each artist has for their chosen material.

I have returned several times to the idea that, for these artists, 'nature' is an all-encompassing concept, describing the essence and the cosmos, the micro and the macro. 'The quality that we call beauty...must always grow from the realities of life.'[23] When Chiyoko Tanake rubs the sand into her cloth, through her actions she becomes part of the continuum which began with the pebbles rubbing together until they became the sand she is using to re-establish that primal contact with the earth. Susan K. Langer speaks of a space being created by lines which becomes ipso facto a temporal space, that is a spatio-temporal form,[24] equally the continuum of time could also be described as a line, and that line may be implicit. The three woven works, boxed in Perspex, by Naomi Kobayashi are made from torn strips of paper which were originally the papers used by her mother for her calligraphic work, the line of time contained within the work.

If, as Kandinsky famously said, 'A line is a point hurled into space',[25] then the works in this exhibition can be understood as linear constructions. The method of making used by most of these artists is

a line is a point hurled into space - Kandinsky

19 Yasuke Nakahara 'Between Man and Matter' 1970 quoted by Toyojio Hida 'Giving a New Life to Material' Catalogue 16th Biennale Internationale de Lausanne 1995

20 Vladimir Markov 'Texture Material' first published as 'Faktura' by the Union of Youth, St. Petersburg 1914. Translated from the Russian by Maria Laakso

21 Toyojio Hida 'Giving a New Life to Material' Catalogue 16th Biennale Internationale de Lausanne 1995

22 Leon van Schaik Introduction to Ushida Findlay's architecture'. 2G Architecture Review No. 6 1998/11

23 Junichiro Tanizaki 'In Praise of Shadows'. First pub. 1933/34. Translated and pub. Leete's Island Books 1977

24 Suzanne K. Langer Essay No. 4 'Living Form' from 'The Problems of Art'. Pub. Scribner's 1957

25 Wassily Kandinsky 'Punkt und Linier zu Fläche' Vol. 9 Bauhaus-Bücher. First Pub. 1926

線は空間に投げられた点 - カンディンスキー

これらのアーティストたち にとって自然と自然形が如何に重要なものであるかは作品の形にも織り地にも表されている。「時が始まって以来、自然はあらゆる物を加工し、あらゆる材質を作ってきた。地上の生命は絶え間なく変化する材質のカオスである。自然ににこれらの材質を発展させる、独自の恒久不変の技術が備わっている。」[20]自然と密接した生活をおくる日本人は、自然の持つ破壊力も再生力も十分認識している。アーティストは自然の持つこれらの要素に魅了され、それを含有し反映するような作品を創造することを目指している。

自然の素材や原材料、野ざらしの繊維、露わになった構造もアーティストを強く引きつける。「例えば、伝統的な日本の木造建造物では、木の部分はニスを塗らないままにしてある...日本人の感覚では、太陽と気候によって老化したニスを塗られていない木の表面は、より暖かくほっとできるように思えるのである。」[21]観る者は、素材が絵を描く時のキャンバスのように単に表現の媒体になってしまうのではなく、個性を保ち、さらにその個性を強め、しかも、綿や紙やステンレス・スティールのようにその本質的な性質をすべて保持していると感じる。建築家の牛田栄作もこう表現している。「私は、日本文化の特徴の中でも手が加えられていないことに価値を見出す感覚を子供たちに伝えたい。なまの魚、原材料、靴を履かない屋内生活、木の風呂、これらは感覚の鋭敏さやなまの感受性といったものを育んでくれる。」[22]こういった取り組み方で仕上がった作品は、生で精製されていない素材にまでさかのぼるような、説明のつかないエネルギーを持つことになる。

表面の材質は素材の本来の可能性を拡大することにより得られる微妙な調和を強調する。素材を征服するのではなく、一緒に仕事をするという感覚である。素材に敬意を払いつつ作品を制作するということは如何なる素材についても言える。たとえポリプロピレンのように極めて抵抗力があるものを素材とした作品であっても、出来上がった作品を観る者は素材に十分な思いやりが込められていると感じる。異なった色調、もっとも強烈なコントラストが、調和の取れた織り地の柔らかさ、純粋さ、新鮮さ、または乾燥性と一緒になり、出来上がった作品は、それぞれのアーティストが使用した素材に対して持っている親しみと理解とを示す。

私は、これらのアーティストたちにとって、「自然」はすべてを包み込む概念であり、本質と秩序、微少なものと大規模なものとを表現しているという考えを繰り返し述べてきた。「私たちが美と呼ぶ特質は...いつも生活の現実から生まれなければならない。」[23]田中千代子が布に砂をこすりつける作業を行う時、彼女は小石を砂になるまでこすり合わせることから始まる連続過程の一部となる。彼女は小石からできた砂を使って大地との原初の接触を復旧させるのである。スーザン・K・ランガーは、線で作り上げられた空間のことを語る。そのような空間は つかの間の空間であり、それはひとつの時空的形態であり[24]、それと同様に、時間の連続体も線として表現されうるであろうし、その線は内在的であるかもしれない。小林尚美が編んでパースペックスに入れた3つの作品は、彼女の母親が書道の作品を書くのに使った紙を細片に裂いて作ったもので、その作品には時間の線が含まれている。

かつてカンディンスキーが言ったように、「線は空間に投げられた点」[25]であるとすれば、この展覧会に出された作品は線を使った三次元の芸術作品だと考えられる。これらのアーティストのほとんどが、線や点を使って作品の内部構造を作り上げるという制作方法を採用している。この仮想空間の中で、「線は動きと休止の両方を表す。仮想空間は純粋な創作作品であるから、それを明確に表現する線は、動きと休止の両方を作り出し、しかも、この二つを同時に作り出す。」[26]組み立てのプロセスがリズムを設定し、そのリズムは、構造によって作り出された空間のリズミカルな活動とぴったりと一致した観る時のリズムにつながる。小林正和が使っている線の中に含まれるエネルギーは、作品を観る者に対して如何なる出発点も終結点も与えることはなく、不変の原動力感を与える。「（一本の）線は孤立状態の中で動く点の軌道であり、従って、人間の状況を象徴することができる。一方、線を使った三次元の芸術作品の中では、線はそれ自体やほかの線と交差し、必ず交流する。相互の結び付きを感じさせる。力を合わせて働く小集団が持つ喜びである。」[27]

これらのアーティストの作品は本質的に構造的なものであって、制作のすべての段階を通して三次元的であるとみなされ、理解されている。ヘンリー・ムーアは「構造は空間であり、観る者はその中を見回すことができる。それによって形は空間的実在となる。」[28]と

20 Vladimir Markov著「Texture Material」「Faktura」として1914年にthe Union of Youth, St. Petersburgが発行。Maria Laaksoがロシア語より英訳

21 Toyojio Hida著1995年第16回ビエンナーレ展カタログ「Giving a New Life to Material」

22 Leon vanSchaik著「Introduction to Ushida Findlay's architecture」2G Architecture Review No.6 1998/11

23 谷崎潤一郎著「In Praise of Shadows」1933/34年初版。1977年Leete's Island Booksが英訳版発行

24 Suzanne K. Langer著エッセイNo4「Living Form」。1957年Scribner発行の「The Problems of Art」より

25 Wassily Kandinsky著「Punkt und Linier zu Flache」第9巻1926年初版Bauhaus-Bucher発行

26 Suzanne K. Langer著エッセイNo4「Living Form」。1957年Scribner発行の「The probkems of Art」より

27 Jane Kaplos著「The Age of Inter Weaving the world: contemporary art of linear construction」1999年横浜美術館発行

28 Henry Moore著「The Sculptor Speaks」。1937年8月18日発行の「Listener」より（Herschell B. Chipp「Theories of Modern Art」1968年University of

one of taking that line, that point and using it to create the internal structure of the work. Within this virtual space 'lines express both motion and rest; and as virtual space is a pure creation, the lines that articulate it create both motion and rest and, moreover, create both at the same time.'[26] The process of construction sets up a rhythm, which leads to a rhythm of looking which exactly corresponds to the rhythmic occupation of space created by the structure. The energy contained within the lines used by Masakazu Kobayashi provides us with no starting point and no ending point but with a sense of a constant dynamic. '(A) line is the track of a point moving in isolation and can thus symbolise the human condition. Yet in art works of linear construction, line intersects with itself or another, there are always interactions. A sense of inter-connectedness arises: the pleasure of elements working co-operatively.'[27]

The work of these artists is essentially structural, conceived and understood to be three dimensional throughout all the stages of making. Henry Moore said that 'the structure is a space within which the eye can move, giving the form a spatial existence.'[28] and for the artists in TEXTURAL SPACE the structure and the space the work will occupy are inseparable elements in its realisation. The means of creating this structure is largely incremental, either as an accumulation of texture or as a multiplication of parts. Yoshiko Tanabe's 'Endless Netway' directly mirrors the natural multiplication of cellular structure, Shigeo Kubota's flat strips, when sewn together, take on three-dimensional form. Harumi Isobe's dense pleated tapestry and her transparent pieces demonstrate a certain polarity between the first, which contains within its structure so much more than is revealed, and the second, which allows us to see through it, revealing more than it contains. '(A) major characteristic of things made from woven fibres is our ability to see through them. We can see both the front surface of a net and that which is on the other side of it, just as light and shadow move freely between the intervals of the weave. This process creates a strange space, one rich in illusion.'[29]

Some of the works accompanying this exhibition have been specially commissioned for specific non-gallery spaces. However it is possible to say that all the work is site-sensitive because each work will be created anew at each venue, setting up a distinct relationship with each space. It can be said that architecture is never final, similarly the works in TEXTURAL SPACE are never 'final' but are re-formed in relation to each particular space, the one influencing the other. Different buildings, different light, different ambient texture, all provide us with a changed perception of both the space within the work and, more particularly, its surrounding space. 'As in rhetoric, where punctuation can be used in the name of silence rather than meaning it, so the built frame can allow us to hear the geography that runs outside it, silently'[30]

During the twentieth century, in the West, the notion gained credibility that the knowing insight of the untutored eye, for whom skills are an irrelevance, has revelatory value. For these Japanese artists it would be considered inappropriate for skills to be separated from the quality of aesthetic experience. The finished pieces are dependent upon the highest level of material understanding, of accumulated skills and knowledge. The concerns are with the beauty of studied simplicity and harmony with nature; 'a preference for internal grace as opposed to external splendour.'[31] Their work presents a collective condition of harmonised colours, lines, textures and forms which serve to transcend genre. There is no necessary correspondence between the most experimental work and novel materials, although there can be. It is the sense of appropriateness which governs the choices, bringing together in a symbiotic relationship, established ways of working with the most original applications and innovations; following the rules and observing norms to perfection, then breaking or moving away without losing contact with their original meaning.

Lesley Millar
Curator Textural Space

the structure is a space within which the eye can move - Henry Moore

[26] Suzanne K. Langer Essay No. 4 'Living Form' from 'The Problems of Art'. Pub. Scribner's 1957

[27] Jano Kaplus 'The Age of Inter', 'Weaving the World: contemporary art of linear construction'. Pub. Yokohama Museum of Art. 1999

[28] Henry Moore 'The Sculptor Speaks' from 'The Listener' 18/8/37. Herschell B. Chipp 'Theories of Modern Art' Pub. University of California Press. 1968

[29] Hideko Numata. Introduction to 'Weaving the World: contemporary art of linear construction'. Pub. Yokohama Museum of Art. 1999

[30] Bernard Cache quoted in 'Truss House Wall'. 2G International Architecture Review No.6 1998/11. Ushida Findlay's Architecture.

[31] 'Japan's Cultural History: A Perspective'. Pub. Ministry of Foreign Affairs, Japan 1973

構造は空間であり、観る者はその中を見回すことができる。それによって形は空間的実在となる。[1]
ヘンリー・ムーア

言っており、「素材空間」のアーティストたちにとって、構造と作品が占める空間とは、作品を形にするときに不可分の要素となっている。この構造は織り地を積み重ねたり、または部分を繰り返したりして作り出されるもので、主に増殖的過程を通して作り出される。 田辺由子の「終わりのないネットウェイ」は細胞組織の自然増殖をかなり忠実に表現したものであり、また、久保田繁夫は平らな細片を縫い合わせて三次元の形を創り出した。磯部晴海による入り組んだ襞をつけたタペストリーと透明な作品を観ると、両作品の間にある種の対極性があることが判る。つまり、前者はその構造の中に外から見えるもの以上にずっと多くのものを含んでいるが、後者の場合は見通すことができるため、作品が含有しているものよりも多くを見せている。「織った繊維で作られたものの主要な特徴（の一つ）は、私たちがそれを見通せるということである。私たちはネットの前面もその反対側にある物も見ることができるが、それはちょうど光と影が織物の間を自由に動くのと同じようである。このプロセスは幻影に富んだ奇妙な空間を作り出す。」[29]
この展覧会に出展された作品の中には、ギャラリーではない場所に置くよう、特に依頼されて作られたものもある。しかしながら、すべての作品が、それぞれの現場で改めて創作され、それぞれの空間と独特な関係を作り上げるのであり、従って、いずれの作品も場所に敏感であると言える。 建築物は決して最終的ではないと言えるし、同様に「素材空間」の作品も決して「最終的」ではなく、それが特定の空間に置かれる度に、その空間と相互作用しながら再形成されるのである。建物、光、環境が変わる度に作品内の空間と、とりわけ、そのまわりを取り囲む空間の両方についての観る者の認識が変化する。「書き言葉では句読点が沈黙を意味するよりも、むしろ沈黙自体を表すことがあるのと同じく、組立てられた枠組があることによって私たちはその外側を動く地理学を静かに聞くことができる。」[30]

二十世紀の西洋では、訓練を受けていない目でも鋭い洞察力さえあれば啓示的才能を発揮することができ、その場合は技量は必要ないという考え方が優勢となった。日本人アーティストなら、技量なしに卓越した唯美的経験をすることなどできないと考えることであろう。彼らの場合、素材に関する豊かな知識、卓越した技量及び知識があって始めて作品が完成する。練り上げた結果得られる単純美、しかも、自然との調和を成した美を創り出そうというのが彼らの願いである。「外観の華麗さではなく、内部の美しさを選好」[31]するのである。彼らの作品は、色、線、織り地、形の集合的調和を表現したものであり、ジャンルを超越した美である。最新の素材を使ったからといって必ずしも最も実験的な作品ができるとは限らない。妥当性というのが彼らの選択基準であり、確立した作業方法での奇抜な応用や革新を目指している。つまり、ルールに従い、完璧を達成するための規範を守り、その上で当初の意図を見失うことなく創作の世界を広げて行くのである。

レズリー・ミラー
素材空間館長

[29] スマタヒデコ「Introduction to Weaving the World: contemporary art of linear construction」1999年横浜美術館発行

[30] Bernard Cache「Truss House Wall」2G InternationalArchitecture Review No.6 1998/11の中で引用

[31] 「Japan's Cultural History: A Perspective」1973年日本外務省発行

fibreworks or textile art of Japan: the historical and contemporary context

Takeo Uchiyama

In America and Eastern Europe during the early 1960's a new type of work emerged in the world of tapestry. This new work transcended the traditional concept that tapestry should be two-dimensional and displayed on a wall, emphasising the texture of yarn or textural structures rather than weaving minutely after designs. These evolved into relief-like and three-dimensional works, through which the wall behind could be seen, works not hung on the wall but suspended in space, placed on a pedestal or directly on the floor like a sculpture. It became difficult to call these new type of works with fibrous materials simply tapestries. The works did not deal with materials or techniques associated with weaving with yarn or looms in the traditional way. Not only yarn but a variety of materials were used such as cords and ropes, unspun fibre, strips of barks and pieces of wood, animal skins and furs, feathers and even wire and metal pieces. Technically, works were not loom-woven and besides knitting and basketry techniques, every possible technique was applied such as binding, tying and winding. These works secured acceptance at the International Biennale of Tapestry in Lausanne, Switzerland, established for the creation of new tapestry as advocated by Jean Lurcat, and became a worldwide trend in the 1970's. However, it was difficult to categorise these works within the traditional sense of tapestry; the terms "fibrework"or "fibre art" were applied but even these new terms are seldom used today.

These fibreworks emerged in Japan in the 1970's. Earlier examples were relief-like, produced in the late 1960's by Hiroshi Awatsuji, a designer of printed interior fabrics, who subsequently pursued works in the design field for which he had originally aimed.

The National Museum of Modern Art, Kyoto, presented *New Textile Artists* in the summer of 1971. This exhibition introduced diversified aspects in the world of textiles at that time; from dyeing and weaving works that emphasised the techniques of traditional crafts. These included designs for printed fabric, rugs and tapestries, dyeing and weaving as an art, even including those works which later will be called fibreworks. The exhibition presented three artists of new textural forms, Toshiko Takagi[1], Emiko Tokushige[2] and Toshiko Horiuchi[3].

Toshiko Takagi[1] had been exhibiting brocade tapestries at the Nitten (Japan Art Exhibition) since around 1940 but from the mid 1960's she started to produce three-dimensional works by combining different woven fabrics. The Japan Art Exhibition was established by the Ministry of Education in 1907, following the example of the salon in France, and it placed importance on fine arts such as *Nihonga* (Japanese-style painting), *yoga* (Western-style painting) and sculpture. Crafts were added in 1927 and as the naming of Craft Art Section indicates, crafts at the Japan Art Exhibition placed more importance on an "aesthetic" rather than a "functional" element, aiming at gaining a status equivalent to painting and sculpture. Thus it was no wonder that Takagi arrived at producing three-dimensional works separately from the new type of textural works abroad. Other textile artists of the Japan Art Exhibition at this stage were still producing two-dimensional tapestries.

It was in 1970, a year before the exhibition, *New Textile Artists*, when Emiko Tokushige[2] presented three-dimensional fibreworks at her one-person exhibition. 1970 was also the year when Toshiko Horiuchi[3], who had been active in America after studying at the Cranbrook Academy of Art, Michigan, returned to Japan. Masakazu Kobayashi[4], Naomi Kobayashi[5] and Tetsuo Kusama, whose works would be accepted at the International Biennale of Tapestry in Lausanne later and become active internationally, exhibited their three-dimensional works with fibre in 1971. Thus it can be said that the development of fibreworks in Japan started about 1970.

Such fibreworks secured the worldwide recognition at the International Biennale of Tapestry in Lausanne which was set up in 1962 by Jean Lurcat and others

日本のファイバーワーク、テキスタイル・アート

内山　武夫

■タピストリーの世界に、図様を精緻に織り上げるのではなく、糸の質感や織組織自体に発言させる作品や、平面で壁に掛けられるものという従来のタピストリーの概念を超えた作品がアメリカや東欧に生まれたのは1960年代の初めだった。やがてレリーフ状の作品から立体的作品、また作品の背後の壁が作品を通して見えるものや、壁に掛けられるのではなくて空間に吊るされたり、彫刻と同様に台や床の上に置かれる作品が創り出されるようになると、それら糸を素材とした新たな造形をタピストリーという言葉で呼べなくなった。また素材や技法の上からも、従来の糸や機で織ることから離れた作品が生まれるようになった。素材として糸だけでなく、様々な紐やロープ、紡がないままの繊維、樹皮や木片、皮革や毛皮、羽根、さらには針金や金属片などが用いられるようになった。技法面では、機で織るのではなくて、編物の技法や籠を編む技法の他、括ったり、縛ったり、巻きつけたりといった、あらゆる技法や手法が用いられるようになった。こうした造形は確かに従来のタピストリーの世界に生まれ、ジャン・リュルサが提唱した新しいタピストリーの創造を目ざして創設された、スイス、ローザンヌの国際タピストリー・ビエンナーレに認知されて、70年代には世界的な傾向となったものだが、従来のタピストリーの語では律し切れなくなったために、これらの造形に対して、「ファイバーワーク」とか「ファイバー・アート」という語が生まれたが、今日ではもう余り用いられなくなっている。

日本でこうした「ファイバーワーク」と呼べる作品が生まれてくるのは1970年頃のことである。インテリアのためのプリント布のデザイナー粟辻博が60年代後半にレリーフ状の作品を創った早い例はあるが、その後粟辻は彼本来のデザインの仕事に専念して行った。

1971年の夏、京都国立近代美術館で『染織の新世代』展を開催した。同展は、その時点での染織界の様々な様相、つまり伝統工芸としての技術を重視する染めや織り、プリント地やラグや壁掛のデザイン、アートとしての染めや織り、さらにのちにファイバーワークと呼ばれるような作品までを紹介するものであった。この時、新たな糸の造形作家として高木敏子[1]、徳重恵美子[2]、堀内紀子[3]の3人を取り上げた。

高木敏子[1]は、日展に1940年頃から綴織の壁掛を出品してきた人であるが、60年代の半ばから織られた布の組合せによる立体的作品を制作するようになっていた。日展はフランスのサロンにならい1907年に文部省によって設立された文展の流れを汲む展覧会で、文展が改革された帝国美術院主催の、いわゆる帝展に工芸が加えられたのは1927年のことで、美術工芸部と称されたことが表すように、日展の工芸は「用」よりも「美」を重視し、絵画、彫刻と肩を並べることを目標とするから、海外の織の新造形とは別箇に、そうした立体的造形に至ったとしても不思議ではないのだが、この段階では日展の他の織作家たちは平面的な壁掛けに止まっていた。

徳重恵美子[2]がファイバーの立体作品を個展に発表したのは、「染織の新世代」展の前半の1970年、合衆国のクランブルック・アカデミー・オブ・アーツに学んでアメリカで活動していた堀内紀子[3]が帰国したのも同じ年だった。また後にローザンヌの国際タピストリー・ビエンナーレに選ばれ、国際的に活躍することとなる小林正和[4]、小林尚美[5]や草間テツオらが糸による立体作品を出品したのが1971年という状況であったから日本でのファイバーワークの発生は1970年頃と言える。

こうした糸の造形はタピストリーの復興を唱えるジャン・リュルサを中心として1962年に創設されたローザンヌの国際タピストリー・ビエンナーレを舞台に世界的になったものだが、当初はタピストリー用の竪機もしくは水平機で織られた作品という制限があり、殆んどが著名な画家やデザイナーの図案を織り出したものであった。日本も第1回展から川島織物の村田博三、第2回展から龍村織物の龍村謙、龍村元らが絵画からデザイン化し会社で製作した作品が出品されていた。そして1967年の第3回展から素材や技法の制限がなくなると、作者自身の手による織作品が増えるとともに、作品のレリーフ化、立体化が起こり、ファイバーワークとしか呼びようのない作品の出現が1969年の第4回展で決定的となったのだが、この時も日本からは以前と同様の作品を出品していたのであった。

第5回展には日本からの入選がなかったこともあって、1973年の第6回展に6名もの作家が入選した。国際舞台へのこの突然とも言える日本のファイバーワークの出現が新鮮な驚きをもって迎えられたのである。また日本国内でもこれが刺激となって、糸の新造形を手がける作家が急速に増えた。

who advocated the revival of tapestry. At the beginning exhibits were limited to those woven on vertical or horizontal tapestry looms and most works were simply woven after designs by well-known painters and designers. Japan participated from the first exhibition with a piece designed by Hirozo Murata of Kawashima Textile Mills from a painting, and for the second exhibition, a work designed by Ken Tatsumura and Gen Tatsumura of Tatsumura Art Textile Company. This was also from a painting, and produced by the respective textile companies. However, restrictions in materials and techniques were removed from the third exhibition in 1967 increasing textural works designed and woven by the artists themselves. At the same time relief-like works and three-dimensional works were shown. Works which could be defined only as fibreworks clearly emerged at the fourth exhibition in 1969 but Japanese participants still exhibited the same works as before.

No works from Japan were accepted at the fifth exhibition but exhibits by six Japanese artists were accepted at the sixth exhibition in 1973 thereby precipitating a sudden emergence of Japanese fibreworks into the international limelight to the surprise of the European audience. The recognition of Japanese artists at this exhibition inspired other Japanese artists, causing this new type of work to increase rapidly.

These new fibreworks gave textiles an independence from painting. This was not an issue found in textiles alone but a movement which could be observed in various fields of crafts since the 1950's.

The field of ceramics became the forerunner of the contemporary transformation of the concept that crafts are equal to fine arts in America and Japan. The signs of the forthcoming tide were found on the West Coast in the mid fifties and Peter Voulkos, who moved from painting to ceramic works, was a leader. His powerful works, which were inspired by Japanese folk craft pottery, stimulated and thereby produced many artists who chose ceramics as the medium to express themselves. Their new ceramic works were called Abstract Expressionist ceramics in the manner of Jackson Pollock and de Kooning whose works, created from the marks of their lives, were called Abstract Expressionist painting. These ceramic works strongly influenced other crafts in America.

About the same time non functional ceramics made as free creations were produced in Japan. The so-called *object* ware produced by artists of Sodeisha, an avant-garde group of ceramic artists in Kyoto, founded by Kazuo Yagi, Osamu Suzuki and others. They were greatly stimulated by ceramic works of Pablo Picasso and Joan Miro and ceramic sculptures by Isamu Noguchi. Thus they distanced themselves from just making vessels in traditional styles, with the result that the barriers between crafts and arts were removed, craftsmen sharing the same issues as artists.

Gobelin tapestry as an art textile started in Japan around the 1890's. It gradually developed and was exhibited at the Crafts Section of the Teiten (Exhibition of the Imperial Academy of Fine Arts) in 1929. The aim was for crafts to gain a status equal to that of fine arts such as painting and sculpture, works worthy to be displayed at exhibitions. Even though Japan had a long history of textiles, there had been no tradition of tapestry, thus from the beginning Japanese artists aimed to produce works unrelated to life, which was different from the situation in foreign countries. From the start the new textile art followed the same path towards art that artistic prints - designed, cut and printed by the artists themselves - had taken before. However, Japanese fibreworks did not originate from the textiles of the Crafts Section of the Japan Art Exhibition which succeeded the Exhibition of the Imperial Academy of Fine Arts. Like the ceramics of the Japan Art Exhibition which still retained the shape of vessels although it advocated beauty free from functionality, textiles of the Japan Art Exhibition in the late 60's produced works in two-dimensional format with their own designs. An exception was Toshiko Takagi[1] who, under the influence of her husband Kazuo Yagi, the leader of Sodeisha, made some daring experiments, but it was a solitary case and she was not followed by others at the time.

A new aspect was incorporated into textiles in Japan during the postwar period as a result of the influx of information and stimulation from abroad and could be seen extensively over the entire world of design. This was related to the Westernisation of Japanese residential space which prompted the emergence of tapestries, screens and rugs that were not mass produced as parts of interior design. Those who met these needs were not the artists of the Japan Art Exhibition who produced traditional art tapestries but those emerging artists who studied new Western aesthetics.

About the end of the 1960's artists who returned from America and Europe after studying textiles started their activities based on the new trends abroad. Works at the International Biennale of Tapestry in Lausanne were introduced by catalogues and the novelty of these new types of textural works caused interest and excitement in Japan. These new trends from abroad greatly influenced the birth of fibreworks in Japan; however, the changes in the concept of crafts which Sodeisha had advocated broke grounds and made the quick acceptance of new trends easier.

Japanese fibreworks in the 1970's were indeed very active and lively. Contrary to the inability of ceramics to break completely away from its own mold - although ceramics was the first genre to break the framework of traditional crafts - the young generation of fibrework artists discarded looms without a second thought and produced works freed from weaving. In contrast to Conceptual Art flourishing at the time, which did not show any trace of artists' hands, these fibreworks showed the joyful marks of the artist's hand. The high evaluation that these works earned abroad accelerated the

こうしたファイバーワークは織の絵画からの独立に他ならない。美術と肩を並べる織の成立とも言える。これは単に織だけの問題ではなく、1950年代以降、工芸の様々な分野に見られる動きであった。

美術と肩を並べる工芸という工芸の変貌の先駆となったのは、アメリカや日本では陶芸の分野であった。アメリカでは西海岸で、1950年代半ばに胎動が始まった。その中心に立ったのは絵画から陶芸に転じたピーター・ヴォーコスであったが、日本の民芸陶器から刺激を受けた力強い彼の作品に啓発されて、自己の表現手段として陶芸を選ぶ作家達が次々と生まれた。彼らの新しい陶芸作品は、ジャクソン・ポロックやウィレム・デクーニングらの生活の痕跡というべき作品が抽象表現主義絵画と呼ばれたのにならって抽象表現主義陶芸と呼ばれたが、これらはアメリカにおいて、他の工芸分野にも大きな影響を与えたのであった。

同じ頃日本でも工芸の用を離れた、自由な造形としての陶芸が生まれた。八木一夫、鈴木治ら京都の走泥社の作家たちの、いわゆるオブジェ焼がそれであるが、彼らはピカソやミロの陶芸作品、イサム・ノグチの陶彫などから多大の刺激を受けつつ、容器を造ることから離れたのであった。このことは工芸と美術の垣根が外され、工芸家も美術家と同じ問題意識を分ち合うようになった結果といえよう。

日本では1890年頃に美術織物としてゴブラン織りのタピストリーが行われるようになり、やがては1927年の帝展美術工芸部の織へと展開して行くのであるが、同展美術工芸部は絵画や彫刻など純粋美術と肩を並べる会場芸術としての工芸を目指したのである。長い織の歴史を持ちながらタピストリーの伝統のなかったわが国では、その成立時から生活と離れたものを目指した訳で、この点外国とは事情が異なり、丁度自画、自刻、自摺を旨とする創作版画と同じような美術への方向を最初からたどってきたといえる。しかし、わが国のファイバーワークは帝展を継いだ日展美術工芸部の織から出たものではない。用から離れた美を主唱しながらも、器形のなごりを残す日展の陶磁器同様、60年代末の日展の織は平面で、独自のデザインを織り出すといった性格のものであった。例外的に走泥社の主導者である夫の八木一夫の影響の下に、高木敏子[1]が大胆な試みを行ってはいたが、当時はまだ他の作家に受継がれることはなかった。

第2次大戦後の日本の織には新たな局面が生まれた。デザイン全体に幅広く見られたように、海外からの情報と刺激によって、それは生まれたのである。それは住空間の西洋化にも関係して、インテリア・デザインの一部として工業製品ではないタピストリー、スクリーン、ラグなどの制作が登場してくるのである。これらを担当したのは既成の鑑賞用のタピストリーを制作する日展の作家たちではなく、西洋的な感覚を学んだ、新たな作家たちであった。

60年代末頃から、アメリカやヨーロッパで織を学んで帰国した作家が、新しい諸外国の動向を基盤とする活動を始めるとともに、ローザンヌの国際タピストリー・ビエンナーレの作品がカタログ等で紹介されるようになって、新しい織の造形の新鮮さが大きな刺激となった。こうした外からの新しい傾向が、わが国のファイバーワークの誕生に大きな影響を与えたのであったが、それらを逸早く受け入れる地盤、つまり走泥社によって起こされた工芸に対する意識の変化があったことを忘れてはならない。

70年代に次々と繰り広げられた、わが国のファイバーによる造形は実に活発であった。工芸の枠を破る作品を生んだのは陶芸の分野が早かったのだが、明確には陶芸の世界を飛び出せていないのとは対照的に、このファイバーワークの作家達は若い世代が主であることもあって、実に自由に機を捨て、織ることにこだわりのない造形を示した。当時の美術界では観念アートが全盛で、作者の手の痕跡を見せない作品が多いなかで、それらファイバーワークの作品はいかにも楽しげな作者の手の動きの痕跡を示していて印象的であった。また海外における評価の高さも、日本のファイバーワークの盛行に拍車をかけた。70年代後半から80年代初めにかけての日本におけるファイバーワークの盛行は、他の諸国と比べても顕著で、特異なものといえるかも知れない。

と言うのは、タピストリーの長く重い伝統をもつヨーロッパではファイバーワークの発生時から批判もあったし、70年代前半にはそれがかなり強まって来た。例えばローザンヌの国際タピストリー・ビエンナーレは新たなタピストリーの創造を目指す場であったのに、新しいアートを生む場になってしまったというような声が強く起こってきた。そして立体的な作品から再び平面作品へと回帰する作家も少なくなかったのである。

1

2

tapestry in Japan was not closely linked to life, the freedom of fibreworks was very alluring

3

popularity of fibreworks in Japan. The thriving of such works in Japan from the late 1970's to the early 1980's was unusually prominent and unique when compared to other countries.

In Europe, with long and substantial traditions of tapestry, there was criticism of fibreworks from the beginning and this was intensified during the first half of the 1970's. For instance, there were some people who were concerned about the direction of the International Biennale of Tapestry in Lausanne, that it had become a place to produce new art although it was originally established for the creation of new tapestry. Thus many artists started to produce two-dimensional rather than three-dimensional works. There was a period in Scandinavian tapestry, which was closely linked to people's lives, when the influence of Polish new textiles was strongly evident, but it did not take too many years before this influence was eradicated. I was often asked by people in European countries in the late 1970's; "Have Japanese works also returned to the two-dimensional?" and they were perplexed when my answer was "It isn't so."

As there has been no firm tradition of tapestry in Japan, there was no home to return to even if we wanted to and as tapestry in Japan was not closely linked to life, the freedom of fibreworks was very alluring. Moreover, in the late seventies a phenomenon occurred that not only woven but also dyed works joined the realm of fibreworks, expanding the range in Japan.

For instance, there are works by Masao Yoshimura which bind layer after layer of cloth together with frayed threads left as they are and works of fraying dyed fabrics by Yushida Teruyoshi. These works were created as responses to the questions, "What is a cloth?" and "What is the meaning of dyeing?" which arose in the world of dyeing. The impetus that included even these works in the category of fibreworks was quite unique to Japan.

The International Biennale of Tapestry in Lausanne opened its doors to dyed works in 1987 and the works by Japanese artists were accepted, such as Shihoko Fukumoto's tie dyed creations Shigeki Fukumoto's wax applications stimulated many young dye artists and broadened the range of fibreworks further. Thus changes in the quality of fibreworks became prominent about this time.

When dyed works were integrated into fibreworks, these were new creations, produced from textiles, which transcended even the new image of fibreworks. Thus the terms "textile art" or "art textile" have been applied. The dyeing techniques and what the artists pursue vary; Shihoko Fukumoto and Shigeki Fukumoto are husband and wife and both have been exhibiting their works at the Craft Art Section of the Japan Art Exhibition. But Shihoko intensified her study of the traditional technique of tie dyeing with indigo. Through her work where many layers of dyed cloth are laid together and hung, she intensified her awareness of space, then expanded it further to the cosmic world. Applying wax with brushstrokes Shigeki, on the other hand, brought a boundless depth to the geometric abstract world created by simple patterns which he assembled into a relief, giving the work further change and depth. Art textiles, dyed works and machine-woven experimental works were accepted at the International Textile Competition, Kyoto, which started in 1987. Works which utilised techniques like screen printing freely were exhibited.

The use of, not only cloth but also paper as a material, is a unique feature of Japanese works and revaluation of paper was intensified in the mid 1970's. The keen interest in Japanese paper shown by artists in other countries, generated stronger interest in paper in Japan. Artists in various fields such as print, produced three-dimensional and installation works utilising paper, works created through paper-making techniques using different materials, and works combining fibre and paper.

生活と密着したタピストリーに特色を見せていたスカンジナビアにも、ポーランドの新しい織の影響が強く見られた時期があったが、それが拭い去られるのに余り年月を要しなかった。70年代後半、ヨーロッパの色々な国の人から「日本でも平面に戻ったか」と聞かれ、「そうでもない」と答えると怪訝な顔をされたものである。

タピストリーの伝統のない日本では戻ろうにも確固とした故郷がないし、日本のタピストリーは生活に密着したものではないから、ファイバーワークの自由さは捨てがたいものなのである。そして70年代の終わりには織の世界だけでなく染めの方からファイバーワークの領域に参画するという現象も起きて、日本のファイバーワークの幅を広げている。

例えば吉村正郎の布を何枚も重ねて截り、ほつけた糸もそのまま呈示する作品や、吉田晃良の染め上げた布をほぐした作品などがそれだが、これらは染色の世界で起こった、「布とは何か」「染めるとはどういうことなのか」といった問いから生まれた作品であると言え、こうした作品をもファイバーワークの世界に包含していく活力は他国に類を見ず、また1987年のローザンヌ国際タピストリー・ビエンナーレでは染作品にも門戸を開き、福本潮子の絞り染めによる作品や、福本繁樹のろう染作品などにも入選したから多くの若い染色家を刺激し、日本のファイバーワークは、更に一層の幅が広がりを示し、このころからファイバーワークの変質が印象づけられるようになったのである。

染めの世界をファイバーワークの世界に取り込んでいくと、このファイバーワークというかつての織から生まれた新たな造形というイメージをも越えた世界が広がってきた。そこでテキスタイル・アートとかアート・テキスタイルと言う言葉が用いられるようになってきているようである。染めの世界からの参入と言っても作家の技法も様々である。福本潮子と繁樹は夫妻であり、ともに以前は日展の美術工芸部に出品していたが、潮子は藍の絞り染の伝統的な技法の研究を深めて、染められた布を何枚も重ねて吊るす作品を契機として空間への意識を深め、更に宇宙へと世界を広げているし、繁樹はシンプルなパターンの型を用いた幾何学的な抽象的世界に撒き蝋を用いて、茫漠とした深さを与え、それをレリーフ状に組合わせて一層の変化と奥行を獲得するというと言うように、染作家の技法も求めるものも様々である。また1987年に始まった国際テキスタイル・コンペティション京都ではアートとしての作品の他、スクリーン・プリントなどの技法を自由に用いた作品も出品されている。

さらに布だけではなく素材としての紙の使用も日本の特色と言えよう。70年代半ばからは紙に対する見直しが日本で高まった。日本の紙に対する外国からの強い注目から、逆に国内の版画家をはじめとする様々なアーティストに、紙に対する強い関心が高まり、紙を用いた立体、空間を占めるインスタレーション的作品を生むに至ったし、独自の素材による紙漉による作品や糸に紙を組合わせた作品が創られるようになった。

この紙に対する関心は1983年に「国際紙会議」が京都で開催されたことが一層の拍車をかけた。紙をテーマとする様々なシンポジウム、ワークショップに加えて、京都国立近代美術館では「新しい紙の美術–アメリカ–」展が開かれ、京都市美術館では「日韓紙造形」展が開かれて、海外の紙造形の状況が生き生きとした形で示され、美術界全般に紙への新たな視点が生まれた。なかでも紙が繊維から成るという親近感からファイバーワークを刺激した点は看過できない。

また染織の織以外の技法、刺繍やレースなどの技法も取り入れられている。まずわが国の刺繍は伝統的には文様をそれを表すにふさわしいステッチによって丹念に正確に刺すというものであったが、織の場合と同様に自由に画家の筆のタッチのように糸を刺すことが行われている。これには英国の50年代以降の刺繍の実り豊かな状況からの影響を見逃せな。80年代初めから、英国のエンブロイダリーを学んで帰国し、活発な活動を示して、日本の伝統的な刺しゅうとは異なる世界を示す作家も出てきたし、京都国立近代美術館が1982年に『イギリスのニードルワーク』展を開催したことも、日本での刺繍に対する新たな可能性を認識させる契機になったようである。同展は英国の17世紀以降の刺繍、ニードル・レース、ビーズワーク、キルティング、パッチワーク、スモッキングに併せて、現代のアートとしてのニードルワークを展示したものであったが、具象的、非具象的を問わず、様々な絵画的意匠を自由に表すイギリスの作家たちの作品に示された針の動きは、見る者に少なからぬ驚きを与えたのであった。

日本のタピストリーは生活に密着したものではないから、ファイバーワークの自由さは捨てがたいものなのである。

4

Such interest in paper was accelerated by the International Paper Conference '83 Japan held in Kyoto. In addition to various symposiums and workshops concerning paper, there were exhibitions such as New American Paperworks at The National Museum of Modern Art, Kyoto and Paperworks of Japan and Korea at the Kyoto Municipal Museum. These exhibitions introduced the state of paperworks in other countries and thereby created a new concept of paper which extended to the whole field of art. The knowledge that paper consists of fibre, further stimulated fibreworks.

Textural techniques, other than weaving, like embroidery and lace have also been incorporated. Traditionally, embroidery has been a technique where a design is diligently and precisely stitched with the most appropriate type of stitches but, in the case of textiles it is now stitched as freely as the touch of a painter's brushstrokes. This was greatly influenced by the very fruitful and successful state of embroidery in England since the 1950's. Artists who returned to Japan after studying embroidery in England emerged in the early 80's, creating works that were different from the traditional embroidery of Japan. The exhibition that The National Museum of Modern Art, Kyoto, organised in 1982, *British Needlework*, helped to make Japanese people aware of new possibilities of needlework. The exhibition presented embroidery, needle lace, beadwork, quilting, patchwork and smocking since the seventeenth century, as well as introducing needlework as contemporary art. The precision of a needle expressing various designs with such freedom shown in British artists' works, whether they were pictorial or non-pictorial, quite surprised and impressed the Japanese viewers.

Works utilising not only embroidery but also lace techniques, began to be produced in the 1970's and early 1980's. These works were created as a result of the stimulation caused by the *International Exhibition of Miniature Textiles* held in London and various cities in the world, and the *International Lace Biennale*. These exhibitions were established as a counteraction to the tendency of works growing to huge sizes. Thus the realm of Japanese textile was broadened even further.

Unlike metals and stones, fibres are organic materials and each different fibre has its own texture and expression. Silk has noble lustre, cotton offers familiarity, while linen has simplicity. Besides such differences in texture, a fibre has the flexibility of a living creature but when it is strung in a straight line it produces clarity. How to use such characteristics of fibre naturally depends upon the concept of each artist. However fibre, a very familiar material to man, together with wood, bamboo and paper, is very well suited to the ethnic sensibility of the Japanese. The use of hard materials often seen in other countries is rare in Japan, with the exception of works by Kyoko Kumai who uses fine stainless steel wire. Traditional European tapestries embody religious, political and social messages and this still continues today. By contrast, generally, the concerns of Japanese artists are directed to the inner world of the individual. An exception is Harumi Isobe[6] who is deeply interested in ecological issues and in her work subtly expresses her concern and anxiety about the worsening environment. Showing the beauty and softness of fibre itself is one of the characteristics of Japanese works. When these are placed amongst works by artists of other countries, the delicate sensibility, serene beauty as well as intimate friendliness become prominent. Many works are light, as if they reject the weight of dignity and power. It is quite surprising that the works of Naomi Kobayashi have the lightness of a fresh breeze from the outdoors or Kyoko Kumai's works are light although she uses fine stainless steel wire and the lustre is not cold but softly embraces the viewer. I have not discussed each artist of TEXTURAL SPACE here but I think none of them deviates considerably from these characteristics of Japanese textile art.

Regardless of its own long tradition of textiles, Japanese fibreworks were created as a result of stimulation from abroad, and have been constantly evolving, incorporating various elements from the world of art and crafts. Even though diverse aspects of fibreworks, which had a vigorous life in many places in the world in the 1970's, have subsided today, Japanese fibre artists are undertaking new experiments and creations.

Takeo Uchiyama
Director
The National Museum of Modern Art, Kyoto

また刺繍だけでなく、レースの技法を新たに生かした作品も行われている。これは作品の巨大化に対する反省もこめて、70年代からロンドンほか世界各地に行われた、国際的なミニアチュア・テキスタイル展や、80年代始めに始まった、ベルギーの国際レースビエンナーレなどが刺激となっている。こうして日本のテキスタイルは増々その幅を広げているのである。

糸という素材は金属や石とは異なって、有機的であり、糸の種類によって、それぞれの表情をもっている。絹には高貴な光があり、木綿には親しみやすさが、また麻には素朴さがあるなどなど。さらにそうした質感だけでなくて、糸には生物のような、しなやかさが備わっているし、また直線に張れば凛とした確かさが生まれる。勿論、このような糸の性質をどのように用いるかは作家個々の造形意志の問題であるが、糸という人と親しみやすい素材は、木や竹や紙とともに、日本の民族性に合っていると言ってよいだろう。諸外国でよく見られた糸以外の硬質な素材の使用は、熊井恭子のようにステンレス・スティールの糸を用いるという例もあるが、一般には余り見られない。しかもヨーロッパの伝統的タピストリーには宗教的、政治的、社会的メッセージが込められており、今もそれが生きているのに対して、日本では磯辺晴美[6]のように環境問題に深い関心を寄せ、控え目に環境悪化への懸念を作品に表す作家もあるが、それは例外的存在であり、一般的には日本の作家たちの作品は個人の内面の世界に向けられていると言えよう。糸自体の美しさ、優しさを強く示す作品が多いのも、ひとつの特色と言えるかも知れない。諸外国の作品のなかに、日本の作品を置いて見たとき、繊細な感性、静朗な美しさと共に親密な優しさが際立つであろう。多くの作品は重厚さや力と言った強さを拒否するかのように軽やかである。小林尚美の作品のように、戸外のさわやかな風のような軽やかさをもっているし、ステンレス・スチールの糸を用いながらも、熊井恭子の作品は軽やかで、その輝きは決して冷やかではなく、優しく見る者を包み込むことには驚かされる。今回の素材空間に出品している作家個々について述べることはしないが、こうした日本のテキスタイル・アートの特色から大きく外れる作家はいないはずである。

染織の長い歴史をもち乍らも、それとは殆んど無関係に、海外からの刺激によって生まれた日本のファイバーワークは、様々な要素を美術や他の工芸から取り入れて、常に変化を重ねてきた。世界の各地で展開された70年代のファイバーワークの様々な状況が沈静化した今も、日本の作家たちは新たな実験と創作を展開しているのである。

内山　武夫
京都国立近代美術館館長

5

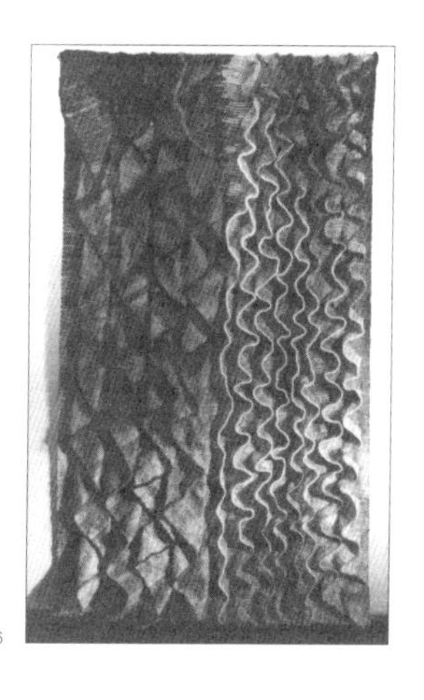
6

contemporary fibre art in public spaces in Japan

Kiyoji Tsuji

A new type of work called fibre art emerged in Japan at the end of the 1960's and started to gain a foothold in the 1970's. The centre of activity moved from Tokyo to Kyoto, a city which has been nurturing traditional textile techniques and materials for a long time. By the mid 1970's Japanese fibre art had entered the international arena through the participation of Japanese artists in the International Biennale of Tapestry in Lausanne, Switzerland, and this new type of art work gradually gained recognition in the domestic art world, particularly in the area around Kyoto. The National Museums of Modern Art in Tokyo and Kyoto presented exhibitions of fibre art for the first time in Japan. Through *Fibre Works – Europe and Japan* in 1976 and *Fibre Works – America and Japan* in 1977 the new genre became widely known to the Japanese public.

Magazines specialising in interior decoration enthusiastically introduced these fibre art works and the architectural world became aware of this new type of work. Interior fabrics (new designs printed on fabric) attracted attention as partitions of space and wall decorations in Japanese architecture and interior decoration. Tapestries gradually started to be incorporated in architecture as wall decoration. Two-dimensional tapestries with a new sense of design, produced by fibre artists, started to adorn architectural space. Soon two-dimensional tapestries evolved into relief-like works which placed more emphasis on the sense of materials or those whose construction was not confined to weaving techniques. The change was brought about through the combination of architects enthusiastically utilising the new designs, together with the particular Japanese sensibility for the feeling of materials.

Socially, on the other hand, Japan was enjoying a good economy and from the end of the 1970's and during the 1980's the local governments throughout Japan established the Architecture One-Percent Ordinance. This specified that when a local government constructs a public building it must allot 1% of its construction budget to artistic enterprises. Early examples of this were "One-Percent System for Culture" by Kanagawa Prefecture in 1978 and "Fragrance of Culture, One-Percent Project" by Shiga Prefecture in 1979. These schemes incorporated artistic and cultural elements into previously standardised and monotonous local government facilities. At the same time there was a vigorous undertaking of exhibition projects by each local government to install art works in public spaces together with a policy of utilising artistic elements in city re-adjustment plans.

As the concept of public art gained ground, corporate bodies, from a position of wishing to contribute to society, began to be actively involved in cultural enterprises. They installed art works on the walls of their offices or converted their showrooms into galleries. The way a corporate body is committed to art and culture influences its corporate image and prestige and this has become an important element in commercial spaces. It is especially noticeable in hotels and other commercial facilities that artistic projects involving art works are becoming indispensable today, relating art projects directly to corporate image and business.

With such development the demand for fibre works, particularly those which are light and can be installed and adjusted easily after construction, has increased. This in turn has led to fibre works growing in scale and thereby gaining opportunities to be installed in public spaces.

By the mid 1980's spatial works (wholly three-dimensional), which dramatised their surrounding space, began to be incorporated into architecture. At the same time legal restrictions were applied to architecture and art work. For example, fibre works adorning the walls and installed after the architecture was constructed, were regarded as accessories like paintings, but spatial works were regarded as part of the constructed architecture.

日本の公共空間におけるテキスタイルアート

辻 喜代治

ファイバーアートと呼ばれる新しい仕事が、日本に登場してくるのは60年代末のことで、本格的に活動を始めるのは、70年代に入ってからである。その中心は、東京からやがて、古くから染織の伝統技術や、素材が受け継がれている京都に移って展開することになる。そして70年代中頃までには、日本のファイバーアートの仕事も、ローザンヌの国際タペストリー展を通じて国際舞台に登場し、国内の美術界、特に京都を中心とする地域で、その新しい仕事は徐々に認められていくようになる。さらに京都と東京の国立近代美術館で、日本の美術館で初めて開催されたファイバーアート展、現代の造形「織り」—ヨーロッパと日本（1976年）、—アメリカと日本（1977年）によって、この分野は広く一般に知られるようになる。

そうした染織の新しい仕事はインテリア雑誌などに積極的に取り上げられ、建築の世界でも、その存在が知られるようになる。当時の日本の建築・インテリア界では、空間の間仕切りや、壁面の装飾としてインテリアファブリック（布にプリントされた新しいデザインのもの）が、注目されていた。そんな中に、壁面の装飾として徐々にではあるが、タペストリーが組み込まれ、ファイバー作家の新しいデザイン感覚の平面タペストリーが、建築空間に登場することになる。やがて平面のタペストリーは、より素材感を強調したレリーフ状の作品や、織の技法にしばられない表現作品へと変化していくことになる。その背景には、競って建築界が、新しいデザインをとり入れていったこと、素材感にこだわる日本人の感性が、強く働いたことがあったと思われる。

一方社会的には、徐々に経済的にもゆとりも生れ、70年代末から80年代にかけて、地方の自治体も公共建築物に、その予算の1％を芸術事業に使用する、いわゆる芸術1％条令が各地で制定されるようになる。その早い取り組みとしては、1978年、神奈川県の「文化のための1％システム」、1979年、滋賀県の「文化の香り1％事業」などがあげられる。それまでの画一的でうるおいのなかった県の施設に対して、芸術文化的要素を取り入れていった。同時に政策として、公共空間に芸術作品を設置する展覧会企画や、芸術要素を使った都市整備計画が、各自治体によって盛んに行われるようになる。

公共芸術の考え方が広がってくると共に、一般企業も社会的貢献の立場から、文化事業に積極的に取り組むようになる。オフィスの壁に美術作品をとり入れたり、ショールームを改装してギャラリー機能を持たせたりすることもおこなわれた。企業が美術や文化にどのように取り組んでいくかが、企業イメージを左右する大きな要因となり、商業空間においても重要な要素となってくる。特にホテルなどの商業施設の、芸術作品を起用するアート計画は、そのイメージ形成と共に経営に直接関係するもので、現在では必須条件となっている。

こうした時代背景の中で、重量が軽く建築後でも取り付けなどの加工がしやすいファイバー作品は、その需要を伸ばし、より大型化し公共的なスペースを獲得していくことになる。80年代中頃には、さらに、空間そのものを演出する空間的（三次元的）作品が、建築の中に取り入れられるようになる。同時に、建築の法的制約が、作品に加わるのもこの時期からである。つまり、それまでの壁面を飾るファイバー作品は、絵画などと同じく、建築後の付属美術品として扱われたが、一方、空間的な作品は、建築に関わる構造の一部とみなされたのである。

そのために日本の消防法によって、ファイバー作品にまず防炎加工が要求され、またスプリンクラーなどの消化設備の位置によっては、空間の作品取り付け場所を変更せざるを得ない場合も出てくる。ファイバー作家たちは、素材メーカーの協力で、新しい素材を開発したり、表面の加工技術を取り入れるなどして、今までに、それらの問題を解決してきている。建築物と作品の関わりにおいては、他に、作品の耐久性や汚れの問題も解決されなければならなかった。現在では作家が、作品売買契約時に作品のメンテナンスや保障期限事項を盛り込み、発注者と互いにファイバー作品独自のあり方を理解して、公共空間に設置されるようになってきている。

こうした作家たちの努力によって、ホテル、商業施設、オフィスビルや、自治体の公共建築物など、多数の空間にファイバー作品が取り入れられるようになった。また、建築費の中に、始めから美術予算が組み込まれた場合には、作家が設計段階から積極的な提案を行い、

This means that under the regulations a fibre work is required to have fireproof treatment and the location of the work to be installed has to be changed at times to accommodate the positioning of sprinklers. Fibre artists have solved these problems by developing new materials with the co-operation of the material manufacturers or by using new techniques of surface treatment. In the relationship between architecture and art works the issues of durability and damage by soiling and pollution must also be solved. Today, at the time of concluding the sales contract, the maintenance and guarantee period of the work are incorporated by the fibre artist and the fibre art works are installed in public spaces with both parties understanding the unique quality of the work.

The result of these endeavours by artists has been that fibre works began to be installed in a variety of spaces. These included hotels, commercial facilities, office buildings and public buildings constructed by local governments. Sometimes when the construction costs includes the budget for art works from the outset, artists actively participate from the planning stage, proposing ideas and giving advice, thus creating a space together with the architect. The flexibility and the sense of material of the fibre works, dramatically changed the blank architectural space produced by the concrete buildings which have emerged in abundance since the 1980's. This has produced a close relationship between fibre works and architecture in Japan, a unique relationship; rare in the world.

Traditional Japanese houses used to be made of natural materials such as clay, wood and paper, composing the entire room interiors. The natural materials used to have special considerations, for instance: for wooden materials, woods with different textures were used subtly to suit the characteristics of each room. With the exception of the traditional Japanese *tokonoma* (an alcove), Japanese housing space basically does not require any decoration such as paintings. The house was a "life space" where people appreciated the unique expression that each material has, its combination and contrast. Today architectural space with fibre works is, in a sense, an embodiment of a spiritual particularity for materials that the Japanese have inherited and have been nurturing.

The tea ceremony is one form of traditional Japanese culture. A tearoom, which is specially designated and designed to prepare powdered green tea, is indeed a creative space produced by this appreciation of the contrast of materials. It is also an imaginary space of nature, created by the natural materials. In the tea ceremony there is *nodate*, a style of making tea outdoors in the fields and gardens. At the flower-viewing time in the spring, a red and white striped fabric encloses a space under a plum or cherry blossom tree, likening it to a temporary tearoom where people enjoy preparing and drinking tea. In this space, defined by the cloth, people can sense the breeze, feel the light and enjoy the world of tea in a natural environment. Historically in the life of Japanese people there has been a culture where fabric, space and nature are integrated.

Masakazu Kobayashi, one of the artists in Textural Space, living in Kyoto, exhibited *Nodate Kurondani 1996*, a *nodate* space in a contemporary sense, at the *Kyoto Arts Festival* in 1996 which was organised by the City of Kyoto. The Festival is an outdoor art exhibition held annually at temples and shrines in Kyoto and Kobayashi won the Grand Prix for his work. In front of the temple gate he constructed a square space, 3.5 metres by 3.5 metres, with white nylon tent fabric, enclosing the existing stone bench. The space was composed of the ground covered with small pebbles, green moss and water. A large circular hole was cut out of the ceiling of the white fabric and the sunlight shone through forming a circle which moved across the moss, making the viewer conscious of the quiet flow of time. Within the white fabric was a landscape which incorporated details of nature, a temple and a gate. The involvement of the viewer moving within the space, and creating a silhouette through the fabric, became an element of the work as a whole. The fabric, nature, space and human elements together created a new form of art. I would like to propose that Kobayashi's work was a textile work in a public space although it was of an ephemeral nature.

I have discussed briefly the historical flow and the present state of fibre and textile art in public spaces in Japan and the important role played by the commissioning of work for architecture in the development of this field. At the same time fibre and textile art have become an important element for architectural space today. As it is becoming increasingly difficult to sell this kind of work through galleries, the increase in demand for textile work in architecture is definitely nurturing and producing new artists in this field. The international competitions such as the Kyoto International Textile Competition and numerous fibre and textile exhibitions in Japan and abroad have been held since the 1990's and it is an art form which shows the most active development in Japan today.

Kyoji Tsuji
Associate Professor
Seian University of Art and Design

建築家と一緒に空間を作り上げていくこともある。ファイバー作品が持つしなやかな素材感は、80年代から多く登場するコンクリートを中心とした無表情な建築空間を、ドラマチックに変化させてきている。こうして現在では、世界ではあまり見られない日本独自のファイバー作品と建築との緊密な関係が、生れることになる。

伝統的な日本の住居はかつて、土、木、紙、などの自然素材を用いて、室内空間全体を構成していた。そこに使われる自然素材には、特別なこだわりがあり、例えば木の素材では、部屋の性質に合わせて、表情の違った木材を微妙に使い分けた。日本人の住居空間は、床の間を除いて、基本的には絵画などの装飾物を必要とせず、それぞれの素材が持つ独自の表情と、その組み合わせや対比を楽しむ生活の空間であった。現代のファイバー作品による建築空間は、こうした日本人が過去に培ってきた素材への精神的なこだわりが、形を変えて、今に受け継がれているのである。

日本の伝統的な文化の中に茶道がある。茶道の舞台となる茶室空間は、まさにその素材感の対比が創り出した創造空間であり、そこに使われている素材から創り出される、自然への想像空間でもある。茶道の世界では、自然の野や庭園において行われる野点といわれる茶会がある。春の花見の時期などに、梅や桜の花の咲く下で、紅白の布で空間を囲い、そこを仮の茶室と見立て、お茶を楽しむのである。人々は布で切り取られた空間で風を感じ、光を感じ、自然空間の中でお茶の世界に興じてきた。日本人の生活の中には、古くから布と、空間と、自然が一体化した文化が存在していたのである。

1996年、京都に住むファイバーアティスト小林正和は、京都市が主催する「芸術祭典・京」の公募展に、現代の野点空間「NODATE KURODANI 1996」を出品した。この展覧会は、古都の寺社を使って毎年開催される野外造形展で、小林はこの作品で大賞を受賞した。作品は寺の山門を背景に、既存の石のベンチを取り込み、真っ白なナイロン素材のテント布を使い、3.5メートル角の空間を構成した。内部には小さな石がひかれ、緑色の苔と、水によって構成されている。白い布で囲われた空間の天井部の布には、大きな円形の穴があけられ、そこから陽光が差し込み、地上の苔の円上を移ろう様に、静かな時の流れを意識させる作品であった。

そこには寺や山門の景色を作品空間にとり込み、白い布で囲われた空間には小さなスケールの自然があり、さらに観者が加わる。その人の動きも布の外側ではシルエットとなり、作品全体の一つの要素となっている。布、自然、空間、そして人間が作り出す、新しい形のアート作品といえる。この作品も仮設ではあるが、公共空間におけるテキスタイル作品として、ぜひ紹介しておきたい。

以上、日本の公共空間におけるファイバーやテキスタイルアートの歴史的流れと現状を述べてきたが、建築のコミッションワークは、この分野の発展に特に重要な役割を果たしてきている。同時に現在では、建築空間にとってファイバーやテキスタイル作品は、重要なエレメントとさえなっているような感じさえ受ける。ギャラリーでの作品販売が難しくなってきている日本では、この建築におけるテキスタイル作品の需要の増大は、確実にファイバーやテキスタイル分野の作家を育成してきた。そして常に新しい作家を生んできた。さらに90年代になって、京都国際テキスタイルコンペティションなどの国際公募展や、国内外での日本のファイバーやテキスタイルの企画展が数多く開催され、現在日本では、最も活発な展開を見せる美術分野となっている。

辻喜代治
成安造形大学助教授

contemporary Japanese textile art in an international perspective

Keiko Kawashima

The development of contemporary textile art in Japan cannot be discussed without reference to the International Biennale of Tapestry in Lausanne, Switzerland, held from 1962 to 1995. Works by many Japanese textile artists were accepted each time since the Biennale became a competition in 1973, and artists of all countries were invited to participate. These works have always charmed people.

Until then the techniques in dyeing and weaving, which were introduced to Japan via the Silk Road, China and Korea, had shown indigenous development in Japan through the donning of the kimono, the traditional Japanese clothing. However the world of textiles showed quite a drastic development in the 1970's with the influence of American Abstract Expressionism and the activities of Japanese artists who returned from studies in Europe.

The works by Masakazu Kobayashi, Naomi Kobayashi, Chiyoko Tanaka and Kyoko Kumai, the participants of TEXTURAL SPACE, were accepted at the International Triennale of Tapestry in Lodz, Poland, which became an international exhibition in 1975. The Art Gallery of Western Australia organised and presented an exhibition of Japanese fibre art at the First Perth International Crafts Triennale in 1989 and subsequently several exhibitions of miniature textile art were held at various parts of Australia. Interest in Japanese textile art continues today. In the 1990's American curators organised many exhibitions of Japanese textile art, for instance, *Light and Shadow Japanese Artists in the Space* at The North Dakota Museum of Art in 1993 and 1994 and *Structure and Surface –Contemporary Japanese Textiles* at The Museum of Modern Art, New York in 1998. Many Japanese textile artists have been accepted and have won awards at international competitions abroad.

The above exhibitions helped to develop the unique non functional Japanese textile art, while making sure that traditional techniques were not forgotten. Furthermore, the unique sense of space peculiar to the Japanese is incorporated in this work which is known to excite people in foreign countries.

many Japanese textile artists have won awards at international competitions

日本のコンテンポラリーテキスタイルアートの国際性

川嶋 啓子

日本のコンテンポラリーテキスタイルアートの発展は、1962年から1995年まで、スイスのローザンヌで開催されていたローザンヌ　タピストリービエンナーレを抜きにしては、考えられないでしょう。この展覧会が公募制になった1973年から、毎回、多くの日本作家達の作品が入選し、その作品群は多くの人々を魅了してきました。それまでにも、日本においては、古来より着物を着ることによって、遠くは、シルクロードや中国大陸、朝鮮半島を経由して入った染め、織の技術は、独自の発展を遂げてきましたが、1970年代に入り、アメリカの抽象表現主義の影響やヨーロッパへの留学から戻ってきた作家達によって、テキスタイルの世界も一挙にこれまでとは違った発展を遂げる事になります。

また、1975年度から国際展になったポーランドのインターナショナル タペストリー トリエンナーレでも、小林正和、小林尚美、田中千世子、熊井恭子といったTEXTURAL SPACE展に出品している作家たちが、入賞していますし、1980年代後半になると西オーストラリア州立美術館が、"第１回パース　インナーナショナルクラフト　トリエンナーレ展(1989年）で日本のファイバーアートの展覧会を企画し、その後オーストラリア各地において、ファイバーアートのミニアチュール展が数回に渡って開催され、現在でもその交流は続けられています。1990 年代に入ると、アメリカにおいてノースダコタ州立美術館での "光と影(1993年と1994年）"や、ニューヨークの近代美術館での"現代日本のテキスタイル(1998年)など、日本のテキスタイルアートの展覧会を多くの海外のキュレーターが企画してきました。また、日本のテキスタイルアートは、今なお、他の国々で開催される国際的な公募展においても、多くの入選者や入賞者を出しています。

つまり、それは日本独自のテキスタイルアートへの発展をうながしました。着物ではなく、また使えるファブリックでもないアートの世界です。しかし、そこには、本来の伝統的な日本の染織の技術も忘れられてないと思います。そして、日本独特の空間感覚が入り込み、海外の人々を魅了するテキスタイルアートが形成されていると私は思っています。

その日本独特の空間感覚について少し述べたいと思います。私たち日本人は、日本の気候にあった建築物として木造の住居に住んでいます。今現在では、西洋と

日本の織物アーティストたちは，織物の材質について私たちが期待する点を疑問視している。

the Japanese
are very used
to thinking about
objects adorning
the space as
three-dimensional,
not simply
two-dimensional

I would like to touch briefly upon this unique sense of space which is peculiar to the Japanese. We have been living in wooden houses which are best adapted to Japanese climatic conditions. However, people living in Western-style apartments are increasing today. Until quite recently most houses were constructed with wood. Traditional Japanese houses are constructed with wooden columns and the interiors are divided into rooms by mobile sliding screens and sliding doors, *shoji* and *fusuma*, instead of immobile walls. It is quite different from the stone and brick walls used in Western architecture. The floors of the interior of the houses are covered with *tatami* mats. The columns that support the structure also the sliding screens and sliding doors are made of wood and paper. Rushes (*igusa*), a plant, are woven to make *tatami* mats and it is no exaggeration to say that our living space is surrounded by fibre. This is quite different from the interpretation of fibre in oversea countries.

Japanese textile art has been influenced by this unique sense for our living space which is infused into the Japanese regardless of whether artists are conscious of it or not. We feel very familiar with not only fabrics but other fibre materials such as paper and wood and these materials make our life more comfortable. Perhaps the reason why European people find Japanese textile art fascinating is derived from this. European people produced tapestries to decorate stone and brick walls which are cold to the touch. Japanese textile art has a different feeling. The difference in the wall structures, caused the Europeans and the Japanese to produce different developments in textile art. In our everyday experience the Japanese are very used to thinking about objects adorning the space as three-dimensional, not simply two-dimensional.

For instance, kimono, woven as fabric and simply sewn together, seems at a glance like an ordinary cloth when folded, but it quite beautifully wraps up a three-dimensional human body. It is quite different from Western clothes.

This unique sense of space peculiar to the Japanese that we have been nurturing for a long time has produced the development of contemporary Japanese textile art in the international arena. International recognition in the end depends on how well the Japanese identity and the individuality of the artist are incorporated together.

The artists in TEXTURAL SPACE first studied the traditional techniques of Japanese textiles and incorporated them with their own sense of space, thereby creating their innovative works with originality, making their works more fascinating internationally.

Despite the works of many Japanese artists appealing to people overseas, the interest that scholars, funding bodies and others in Japan have shown is slight compared to the greater extent of interest from the West. Although TEXTURAL SPACE, has the cooperation of a few scholars and funding bodies in Japan, it is made possible by tremendous efforts on the British side. I sincerely hope that the exhibition nurtures more interest in contemporary textile art in Japan, thereby producing more scholars and corporate bodies who are sympathetic to this form of expression.

Finally I would like to express my gratitude for being given this opportunity to help in this exhibition and to have experiences which have prompted me to think about Japanese textile art from an international perspective. I also would like to express my highest esteem for the artists, as well as Lesley Millar and the many people who have worked and put their best efforts into realising this exhibition.

Keiko Kawashima
Exhibition Co-ordinator in Japan
Director, GalleryGallery
Director, Kyoto Contemporary
Textile Art Center (KICTAC)

同じようなアパートメント形式の住居に住んでいる人々も多く見られますが、少し前までは、ほとんどが木で建てられた住居でした。それは、木の柱構造で建てられたもので、内部は、障子やふすまといった移動性のあるものが壁の代わりとして部屋を仕切っています。西洋で見られる石や、レンガの壁とは大きく異ります。また、床には畳が敷かれています。建築を支えている柱の木は、もちろんのこと、障子やふすまは、木と紙で出来ていますし、畳は植物のい草というものが織られたもので出来ています。つまり、私たちの生活空間が全てファイバーというもので囲まれているといっても、過言ではないと思います。これは、海外で考えられているテキスタイルとは、大きく違ったものではないでしょうか?

日本のテキスタイルアートは、この日本の住空間からの影響が作家を意識しようがしよまいが、私たち日本人の中に入り込んでいるのではないかと私は思っています。つまり、布はもちろんのこと、紙や、木などファイバー素材が、より身近に感じられると言うことです。その素材たちは、私たちの周りを心地良いものにしてくれているのです。ここに、日本のテキスタイルアートがヨーロッパの人々を魅了する一因があるのではないでしょうか？ヨーロッパの人々は、冷たい性質の石やレンガで出来ている壁を装飾するために、タペストリーを制作してきました。日本のテキスタイルアートは、ヨーロッパの人々がタペストリーを制作するというものと違った感覚があるのかもしれません。それはまた壁に対する意識の違いがテキスタイルアートの発展をより違ったものにしました。つまり、私達は、空間を装飾するものを平面的に考えるのではなく、いきなり３次元のものから考えるということを日常的に行っていると言うことではないでしょうか？

たとえば、布として織られ、直線で縫いあわされただけの着物が見ただけではただの平面的な布のような形態であるのに、実際は、立体的な人間の身体をうまく包み込めるものであるというのは、西洋のものとは、大きく違っています。こういった古来から続いている日本独自の空間感覚が、現代の日本のテキスタイルアートを国際的に発展させた要因になっていると思います。国際的な発展とは、結局は日本人としてのアイデンティティと作家独自の個性がうまく重なり合っているか否かということではないでしょうか?

今回TEXTURAL SPACEに出品する作家達も、日本の伝統的な染織の技術を学び、それと、自分の中に存在する空間感覚をうまく融合させ、その作品制作過程においてオリジナルなものを作りあげています。それが、国際的に見ても、作品を魅力的なものにしているのだと私は思います。

多くの日本の作家達の作品が、海外の人々を魅了しているにもかかわらず、日本国内においてその魅力を感じとっている学識者、企業、その他の人々の数は、海外からの興味の大きさに比べると何とも小さいものだと私は感じています。今回のこのイギリスでの展覧会も、数少ない日本の学識者、企業、関係者の協力はあるものの、その多くはイギリス側の莫大な努力によってなりたっています。この展覧会が開催される事により、日本国内においても、日本のコンテンポラリーテキスタイルアートの世界への興味がもっと広がり、専門の学識者や、理解する企業などが、より多く現われる事を願っています。

最後に、この展覧会開催にあたって、お手伝いをさせて頂いたことは、私にとっても日本のテキスタイルアートの国際性を考える良い機会となりました。また様々な有意義な経験をさせて頂いた事に対して、作家の方々や、この展覧会開催の為に、努力を惜しまれなかったLesley Miller氏をはじめとする多くの方々感謝すると共に敬意を表したく思います。

川嶋　啓子/日本側コーディネーター

*ローザンヌの展覧会の正式な名称は、英文では14回までは、"International Biennale of Tapestry", 15回目は、"International Lausanne Biennale Contemporary Textile Art"となり、最後の16回目（公募では無く総集編の）"Lausanne International Biennale - Textile and Contemporary Art -"と変っています。

私達は、空間を装飾するものを平面的に考えるのではなく、いきなり3次元のものから考えるということを日常的に行っている。

素材空間

machiko AGANO

the beauty of coral moving in the water or gills gently breathing

ほのかに息づき、水中を揺らめく珊瑚の繊細な美しさがあります。

title: Untitled
materials: Fishing wire, Steel wire & Handmade paper
size: 4m x 6m x 3.5m

■ One of the many artists in the exhibition who trained initially as a weaver, Machiko Agano now works with the most basic of techniques and equipment to create her large, at times monumental, installations. The work is hand knitted, using very large needles, in garter stitch from fishing line, silk and steel wire, with the stitches made in an irregular pattern. Paradoxically, although the work has the appearance of soft drapes and folds, the materials themselves are not soft. The form and tension of the work is created by its particular hang. The installation is fixed at points attached to the ceiling and floor, sometimes a change of texture and weight at the various 'points', through the addition of hand made paper, holds the work in position. The structural core of her work is clearly defined but, the edges less so. The form suggests the space, moving from these very specific reference points towards less well determined boundaries.

The use of light is very specific. When the work is lit artificially, the drama of shadow and light emphasises the structure and re-defines the space. However when natural light is used, the play of light both reveals and conceals, it changes throughout the day constantly transforming the shape and colour of the work. For Agano the materials have a life of their own and initially she felt it important that she used only natural materials like silk and bamboo. Now, however, she has decided that it is not necessary to use 'natural materials to express natural feelings' and she uses different and various materials as appropriate to the space. Agano's preference is for materials of neutral or no colour allowing the colour of the surrounding area to suffuse and permeate the work. The desire is to convey and make visible the delicate feeling of air. Her smaller work in the exhibition, made with bamboo and silk organza, has the delicate beauty of coral moving in the water or gills gently breathing. Agano states that there should be no sense of finality in the work as presented, allowing all elements to, as she says, 'breathe their own reality'.

■ 出典している芸術家には、もともと織り手として研鑽を受けている人が多いのですが、上野真知子もその中の一人です。現在、上野は最も基本的なテクニックと設備を使用し、巨大な展示品を創作していますが、これが上野の今を記念する作品群となるでしょう。これは手編みの作品で非常に大きな針を使い、仕上げラインをガーター編みにしています。絹と針金を使い、不規則なパターンで縫っています。不思議なことに、この作品の見た目はドレープと折り目で柔らかそうですが、素材自体は柔らかくはありません。作品の形ときめの細かさは、その独特のドレープから生まれているのです。展示作品は天井と床の様々なポイントに固定されていますが、手漉きの紙を加えることにより、時には織地の重みが変化しています。作品の中核構造ははっきりしていますが、端の部分は曖昧です。その空間様式は、非常に具体的な基準となる固定ポイントから、曖昧な境界へと移る形をとっています。

照明の活用方法も非常に独特です。人工照明をあてると、光と影のドラマがこの作品構造を際立たせ、空間が更に変化して見えます。しかし、自然光のときは、光の遊びが現れては消え、消えては現れ、作品の形と色彩が一日中常に変化します。上野にとっては、素材自体が生きているのです。もともと上野は、絹や竹のような自然素材のみを使うことが重要だと感じていました。しかし、現在では自然界の思いを表現するために自然素材にこだわる必要はないと思うようになり、空間にふさわしい様々な異素材を使っています。作品の周りの色彩が、作品を満たしながら透り抜けていくように、上野は淡色や無色の素材が気に入っています。周りの微妙な雰囲気を目に見える形で伝えたいのです。展示会に出品する小さな作品には、竹と絹のオーガンザもあります。この作品には、ほのかに息づき、水中を揺らめく珊瑚の繊細な美しさがあります。上野は、展示された作品に終わりはないと言います。上野の言葉で言うならば、すべての要素は「それ自体の現実世界に生きている」のです。

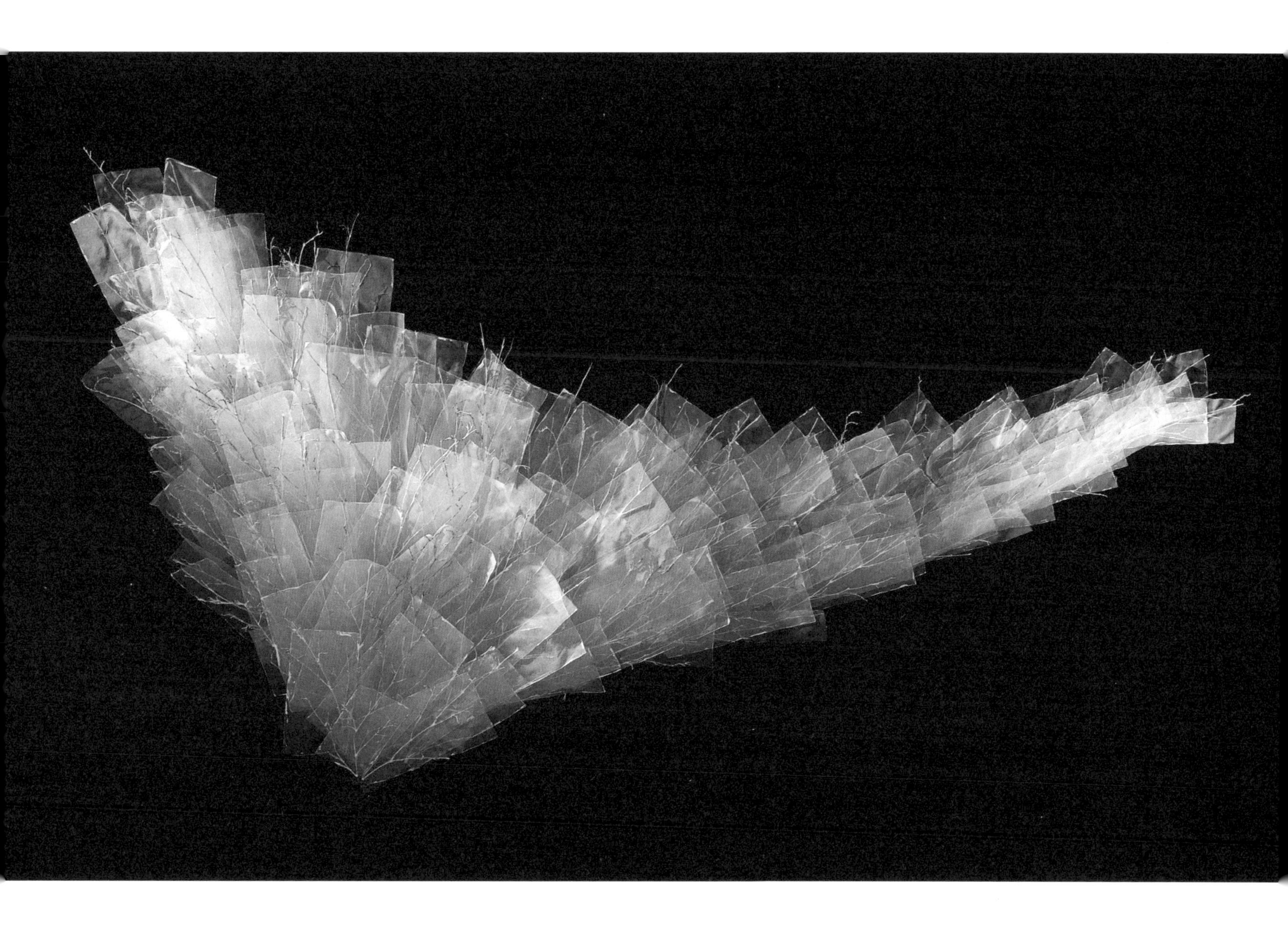

title: Untitled
materials: Silk Organza & Bamboo
size: 2.2m x 1.1m x 0.20m

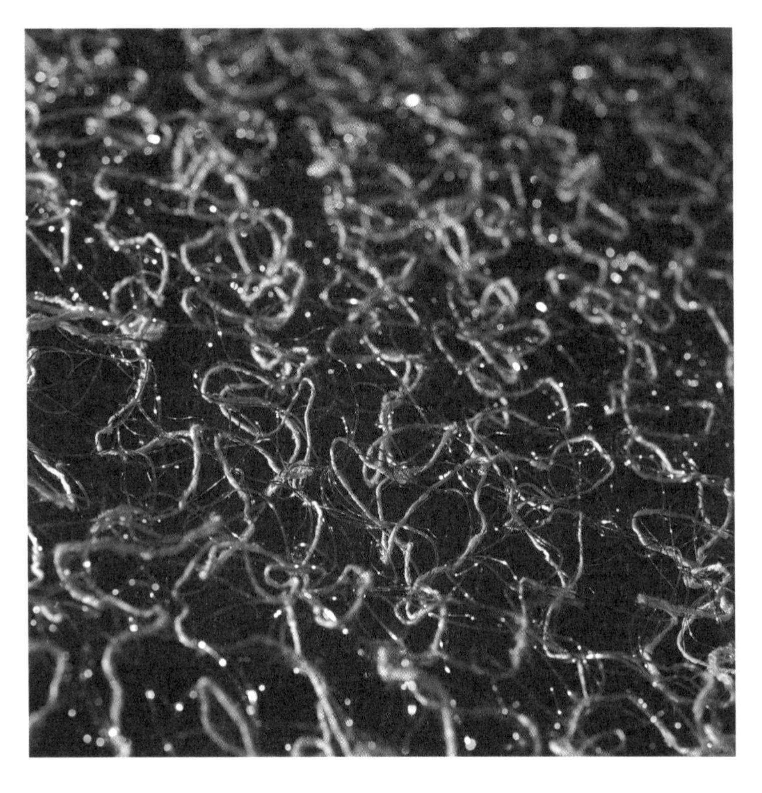

title: Untitled (detail)
materials: Fishing wire & Silk
size: 4m x 6m x 3.5m

title: Untitled (detail)
materials: Silk Organza & Bamboo
size: 2.2m x 1.1m x 0.20m

BIOGRAPHY MACHIKO AGANO

Selected Exhibitions

1983/87/92	Biennale International de Lausanne, Switzerland
	Musee Cantonal des Beaux-Arts, Lausanne
1986	Japanese Contemporary Art Exhibition, Taipei Fine Art Museum, China
1989/98	International Crafts Triennale,
	Art Gallery of Western Australia, Perth, Australia
1991/92	Restless Shadows, UK. tour, 8 venues
1993	Fascinate Textiles, Museum Van Bonnel – Van Dam, Venlo, Holland
1994	Light & Shadow: Japanese Artists in Space,
	North Dakota Museum of Art, USA
1996	Container '96 – Art Across Oceans, Copenhagen, Denmark
1998	Imaginations '98, Gasthuiskapel, Poperinge, Belgium
1999	ITF 6th International Textile Competition, Museum of Kyoto, Japan
2000	The Memories of Algae, Rias Ark Museum of Art, Miyagi, Japan

Public Collection

Kyoto Prefecture
Association Pierren Pauli, Switzerland
The National Gallery of Osaka, Japan
Art Gallery of Western Australia, Perth, Australia
The Museum of Modern Art Gunma, Japan
Rias Ark Museum of Art, Miyagi, Japan

上野真知子

tetsuo FUJIMOTO

■ Tetsuo Fujimoto describes his work as 'machine drawings' which are created by stitch mark on top of stitch mark on top of stitch mark, covering the base cloth and building up an extraordinary surface which ultimately becomes three dimensional. The marks are laid down in a random manner creating a form of impasto or surface layering of lines that build towards the viewer. Such a dense surface texture causes considerable shrinkage, a 5 metre cloth can end up as a 4 metre finished piece. It is important that the work does not lie flat against the wall. For Fujimoto the fold is creating a shadow which is of paramount importance. There is an illusion of depth in his work shaped by the intensity of stitch, by his use of the fold he is presenting us with a three-dimensional reality.

■ 藤本哲夫は自分の作品を「機械による線画」と表現しています。ステッチマークにステッチマークを重ね、立体的になるまで基本となる生地を厚く覆って創作しています。無作為にステッチマークを縫い上げているために、創り出した表層ラインは見ている者の方へ伸びています。このような厚い表層により織物に縮みが生じ、5メートルの布地が仕上がり作品では4メートルになります。この作品は、壁に平坦にかけてはなりません。作品を折ってかけることにより、藤本にとって最も重要な影が生まれるのです。集中的なステッチで形作られた彼の作品には、幻想の深みがあります。折り目を創生し、立体的な現実感を表現しています。

title: Work 98-1 (On Loan From Seiryukai Collection)
materials: Hemp cloth, Polyester threads, Pellon backing & natural plant dyes
size: 3.85m x 1.70m

stitch mark on top of stitch mark building up an extraordinary surface

ステッチマークにステッチマークを重ね、立体的になるまで創作しています。

Fujimoto trained and practised as a weaver for many years, eventually feeling a need to break the tyranny of the vertical and horizontal warp and weft, deciding to experiment with a freer form of expression, closer to the act of drawing. The way of working Fujimoto has devised enables him to have an immediate creative response to the material and an interaction with the texture and the surface.

Initially Fujimoto stitches sub-divisions on the cloth and then 'draws' with the sewing machine, concentrating purely on the texture for at least two months, building stitched mark by stitched mark. After this period of intense sewing, the piece is pinned up on the wall and can be seen as a whole. Another month is then spent pinning the work up and taking it down, making final decisions and adjustments to the density of stitch, weight of colour and movement of light across the work. This way of working has some echo of the weaving of a tapestry on a large loom where the majority of the piece is wound around a roller, only the immediate area on which the weaver is working being visible until the piece is finished, unrolled and revealed.

Fujimoto talks about his work as encompassing the macro and the micro. From a distance the work appears as a dynamic surface, from 2 metres we experience it as an engulfing space and from 15cm we see the intense layering of thread and stitch. He says 'I am now very interested in the fact that the universal macro world and the inner micro world seem to be alike. I am trying to make the macro and micro world coexist in one picture surface, through the linear expression of the sewing machine. The overlapping of lines leads us from the surface to the inner world of that thing.'

藤本は何年間も織り手として研鑽を積んだ結果、垂直・水平の経糸や緯糸の支配を打ち破ることが必要だと感じるようになり、線画に近い自由な表現形式を実験しようと決意しました。藤本が考案した創作方法では、素材と直に創造的な対応ができ、織地や表層と相互作用が生まれます。

藤本は、まず布地をステッチで区分し、次にミシンで線を入れています。2か月間は布地に集中し、ステッチマークの上にステッチマークを積み重ねていきました。この集中的なミシン期間の後に、作品を壁に留めて全体像が見られるようにしました。次の1か月間に作品をピンでたくし上げて壁から外し、ステッチの厚さ、色彩のバランス、作品への光の動きに対して最終調整を行いました。この創作方法には、大型の機織り機で作成するタペストリーの作成方法が投影されています。タペストリーでは作品が完成してロールをほどいてみるまでは、大部分がローラーの周りに巻きつけられているために、織地は織り手の周りしか見られません。

藤本は、自分の作品では巨視的視点と微視的視点が見られると語っています。遠くから作品を見ると、表面はダイナミックに見えます。2メートルのところから見ると、包み込まれるような空間を味わいます。そして、15センチのところから見ると、細かな糸と縫い目が見えるのです。藤本は次のように語っています。「宇宙の巨視的世界と内部の微視的世界が同じように見えるのが、今、非常に面白いと思っている。巨視と微視の世界を、ミシン線の表現を使い、1つの世界の表面に共存させようとしている。線を重ねれば、その作品の表層世界から内部世界へと導くことができる。」

title: Work 99-1
materials: Hemp cloth, Polyester threads, Pellon backing & natural plant dyes
size: 3.13m x 1.75m

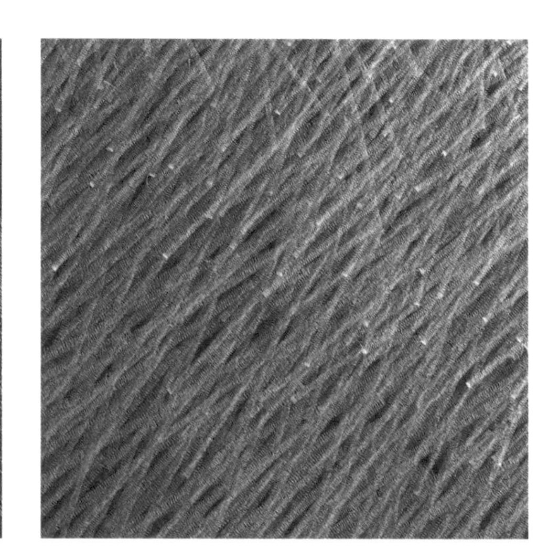

title: Work 98-1 (On Loan From Seiryukai Collection) (detail)
materials: Hemp cloth, Polyester threads,
Pellon backing & natural plant dyes
size: 3.85m x 1.70m

title: Work 99-1 (detail)
materials: Hemp cloth, Polyester threads,
Pellon backing & natural plant dyes
size: 3.13m x 1.75m

BIOGRAPHY TETSUO FUJIMOTO

Selected Exhibitions

1984	Art Now, Hyogo Prefectural Hall of Culture and Art, Japan
	Modern Textilkunst aus Japan Tapisserien und Textilobjekte,
	Museum Bellerive Zurich, Museum of Decorative Art Lausanne,
	Museum Netherland Holland
1987/92	Biennale International de Lausanne, Switzerland
	Musee Cantonal des Beaux-Arts, Lausanne, Switzerland
1991	Kyoto Fibres, Montclair State University & touring U.S.A.
1993	Shiga Annual '93 Fibreworks/The repro-Action of Form,
	The Museum of Modern Art, Shiga, Japan
1996	Japan Textile Exhibition, Meguro Museum of Art, Tokyo, Japan
1997	The Contemporary Stitch: Japan Style
	Montclair State University & touring U.S.A.
1998	ITF the 6th International Textile Competition, Museum of Kyoto
1999	Kyoten Prize: Kyoten, Japan

Public Collections

Japan Foundation, Tokyo
Museum Bellerive, Switzerland
The National Museum of Art, Osaka
The Museum of Kyoto
Wakayama Prefectural Medical College, Wakayama
Kyoto Municipal Museum of Art

藤本 哲夫

shihoko FUKUMOTO

for Fukumoto, indigo is the colour of space

福本にとって、空間の色彩は藍色です。

■ Shihoko Fukumoto originally studied painting, eventually deciding that the painting materials were not suited to her ideas and ways of working. Fukumoto's major concerns are with space and for her indigo is the colour of space. Kyoto has a tradition of indigo dyeing and although her work is strongly contemporary there is also the sense of the continuing tradition which she also acknowledges through her involvement in kimono design. Many of the techniques and tools used by Shihoko Fukumoto are her own invention allowing her to respond intuitively to the possibilities inherent in the dyeing process. Constantly experimenting and testing, each new piece lays down the sources of inspiration for the next. Indigo is vulnerable to sunlight but because light is very important in the understanding of her work she has developed a special technique to prevent it fading. As a natural dye, indigo depends on certain conditions – the air, the weather. The heat and humidity during the summer in Kyoto mean that the winter is the best time for dyeing. In the summer her time is spent assessing work done and thinking about new work.

The methods of indigo dyeing are lengthy, over a period of four to five days the cloth can be dyed several tens of times to reach the required depth of colour, sometimes using several dye baths of differing intensity to achieve the most subtle gradation of dyed colour. The long pieces of linen which comprise the work 'Water-Scape' required the construction of a pulley while they were suspended in the dye vat. After dyeing, heavy brushes were used on the cloth to create the wave effect in the weave. The control needed during dyeing is most evident in 'Opening Moon, Closing Moon' where it was important for extreme care to be taken to avoid staining the white areas with the dye during the rinsing of the cloth.

■ 福本潮子はもともと絵画を勉強していましたが、絵画の素材は自分の創作アイディアや創作方法に適さないと考えました。福本は主に空間に関心があるのです。彼女にとって、空間の色彩は藍色です。京都には藍染めの伝統があります。福本の作品は非常に現代的ではありますが、着物のデザインで培った今に受け継がれる伝統感覚もうかがえます。福本が用いる技術や道具の多くは、自分で考案したものですが、染めの工程独自の可能性に直感的に反応できるような技術や道具です。常に実験とテストを続け、創作した作品は毎回、次回作のインスピレーションの源となっています。藍色は日の光に弱いのですが、日の光は作品の理解に重要であるため、福本は特別な技術を考案して色あせを防いでいます。藍色は自然染料であり、空気や天候などの特定の条件に左右されます。夏の京都は暑くて湿気も多いために、染めには冬が最適です。夏には、今までの作品の評価を行い、新しい作品を考案するのです。

藍染めには時間がかかります。4日から5日間かけ、必要な色彩の深みに達するまで、布を何十回も染めます。時には微妙なグラデュエーションの染め具合を得るために、様々な濃さの染料に浸けることもあります。長い布地の作品は、「水景」を描いています。この作品の創作では、染料に浸け込むことが必要でした。染めた後にどっしりと刷毛をかけ、織布に波模様を創り出します。染めには管理が必要です。「Opening Moon、 Closing Moon」がその良い例でしょう。この作品では、布地をすすいでいる際に白い部分に染料でしみを作らないように、非常に慎重な注意が必要でした。これは、白い部分を1番上にして布を竿から吊るしてホースの水ですすぐことにより、達成できました。作品自体は月の諸段階、最初の展示開始時の月と、展示終了時の月の様子を描いています。「Milky Way」という作品は、多くの小さな正方形のツルファン綿で構成しています。この綿は極めて長い原料繊維であり、作品に類稀なる輝きを与えています。この染めの技術は、「絞り」という伝統手法から、福本自身が開発したバリエーションです。絞り染めとは、折り曲げ、ひだをつけ、縫い込みながら染める手法です。

title: Milky Way
materials: Turpan cotton
size: 2m x 2m

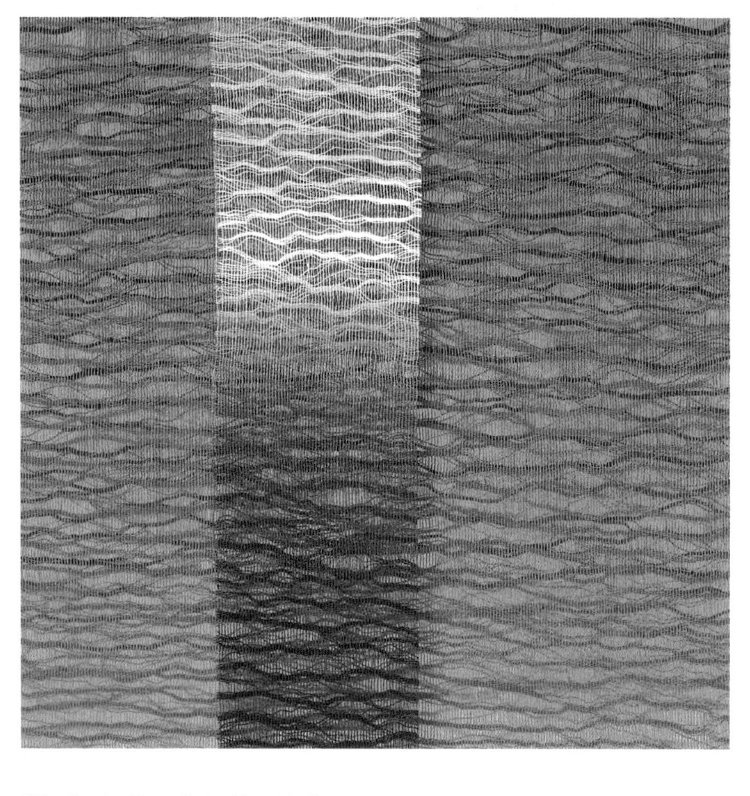

title: Opening Moon, Closing Moon (detail)
materials: Linen
size: each 2m x 2.35m x 0.03m

This was achieved by hanging the cloth on a pole with the white area uppermost and washing it with a shower hose. The work itself depicts the phase of the moon at the time of the exhibition opening and the phase when the exhibition closes at its first venue. The work 'Milky Way' is made from many small squares of Turpan cotton, which has an extra long staple (fibre), giving the work its extraordinary luminousity. The dying technique is Fukumoto's own variation on the traditional method of shibori, a form of tie-dyeing using folding, pleating and sewing.

Fukumoto describes indigo as a 'happy dispensation from nature'. Her inspiration is derived in part from walking the city of Kyoto, its vibrancy and the peace of its temples. The guiding principles behind the work are simplicity, freshness and depth. She says 'when I was young I expressed only simplicity and freshness, as I become older depth is more important.'

福本は、藍染めを「自然からの嬉しい賜りもの」と表現しています。活気ある京都市内や静寂な寺院を歩きながら、福本は作品に対するひらめきを得ます。作品の奥底には、簡素さ、新鮮さ、深遠さがあります。これらの根本的概念が、作品を導いています。福本はこう語っています。「若い頃は、簡素さと新鮮さだけを表現していましたが、年を経るにつれ、深遠さが大切になってきました。」

title: Waterscape
materials: Linen & Indigo
size: Each 1.90m x 4m x 1.70m

title: Opening Moon
materials: Linen
size: each 2m x 2.10m x 0.03m

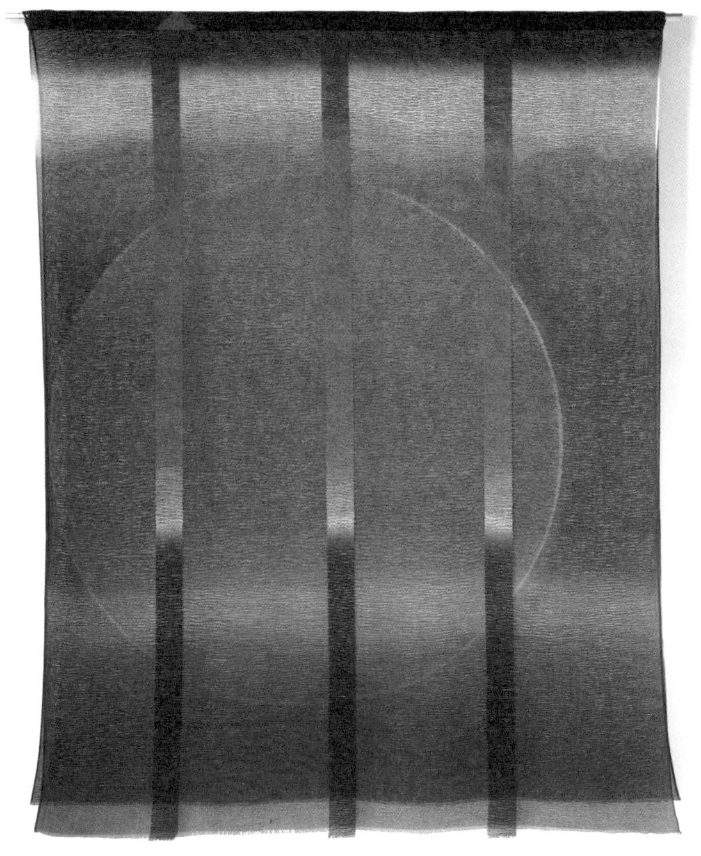

title: Closing Moon
materials: Linen
size: each 2m x 2.35m x 0.03m

BIOGRAPHY SHIHOKO FUKUMOTO

Selected Exhibitions

1986	Indigo: Natural Blue, Royal Tropen Museum Amsterdam, Holland
1987/90/92	Biennale International de Lausanne,
	Musee Cantonnal des Beaux Arts, Lausanne, Switzerland
1990	Solo Exhibition, Rohsska Art and Crafts Museum Gothenburg, Sweden
1991	Dyeing and Weaving. Today's Trends II,
	Gunma Prefectural Museum of Modern Art, Japan
1993	Solo Exhibition, Takashimaya Co. Ltd. Fine Arts Gallery
	New York, Tokyo, Kyoto
1998	Asian Avant-Garde, Christies, London UK.
1999	4th International Tapestry Festival, Bauvais, France
	Invitation Exhibition, Chongju International Craft Biennale, Chongju, Korea
99/2000	50 Masters: 100 Masterpieces from Contemporary Japanese Crafts,
	Paris, Tokyo, Hiroshima, Fukushima, Fukuoka

Prizes and Commissions

33rd Kyoto Craft Exhibition, Grand Prix, Kyoto Prefecture
Kyoto Akebono Prize, Kyoto Prefecture
Takashimaya Art Prize
National Museum of Art, Osaka, Japan
Rohssaka Arts and Crafts Museum, Gothenburg, Sweden
Stanford University Hospital, Stanford U.S.A.
Meijyo University, Nagoya, Japan
University of Chicago, Chicago, U.S.A.
Kyoto Prefecture

福本 潮子

asako ISHIZAKI

the inspiration of the elements - wind, air and light

作品のひらめきのもとは、風、空気、そして光です。

■ Asako Ishizaki trained as a weaver and has developed her own technique and way of working which is a mixture of plain weave and allowing the weft threads to cross freely without warp threads at various points. Once removed from the loom the centre is oversewn to increase the density of the cloth or pleated to give a further dimension. There is a relationship and correspondence between her work and her surroundings in the countryside, which is reflected both in the way in which she considers the ecological implications of her lifestyle and her desire to echo the natural environment within the work. The inspiration of the elements – wind, air and most important, light being her constant theme.

In her piece 'Drawn From Light' the horizontal 'weft' threads have been tie-dyed giving a variation of colour and texture which add to the visual sensation that the work is floating in the air. It is woven from linen, silver yarn and light; the light is used as a component part of the piece. Lit from above the pattern of the threads cast shadows, drawing from the light. 'Field' is placed on the ground. The pleats or folds use light and shadow, holding the form. These are not pieces of cloth cleverly lit, they are textiles which have incorporated light from their inception. The concept of drawing with the light has been the subject of the working method which she has used throughout the whole of the gestation and development of the work, seeing light as not only infiltrating but becoming the strands themselves.

■ 石崎朝子は織り手として研鑽を積み、自分独自の技術と創作手法を開発しています。無地の織物を組み合わせ、経糸を使わずに、様々な箇所で緯糸を自由に交差させるのです。織り機から外した後に、中心部にとめ縫いをして布の厚みを増させる、またはひだをつけて更に立体感を出すのです。その作品は石崎が住んでいる地域の環境と関連性があり、また調和しています。これは、自分の生活様式が生態系にどのような影響を与えるかを考える彼女の考え方にも見てとれます。また、作品に自然環境を表したいという石崎の望みにも表れています。作品のひらめきのもとは、風、空気、そして最も重要なのは、常に作品のテーマともなっている光です。

「Drawn From Light」という作品は、横に伸びる「緯糸」が絞り染めをされており、多様な色彩ときめの細かさを織りなしています。この作品はまるで空中に浮遊しているかのように、視覚に訴えてきます。リネン、銀糸、そして光を織り込んでいます。作品の一部として、光を活かしているのです。糸の上から光をあてると、影が投影されて光が映像を描きます。床に映像を映し出しています。ひだや折り目はその形を保ちながら、光や影を活かしています。これらは光を巧みに外部からあてている布作品ではなく、最初から光を織り込んでいる織物です。光が醸し出す映像という概念は、この作品の考案や創作期間中、常に創作手法の主題となっていました。光を、通り抜けていくものとしてではなく、糸として考えたのです。

title: Drawn From Light
materials: Line & Silver Thread
size: 7m x 2.5m x 1.5m

the concept of drawing light has been the working method

光が醸し出す映像という概念は、常に創作手法の主題となっていました。

title: Field (detail)
materials: Linen, Silk & Bamboo
size: 3.05m x 3.05m

title: Drawn From LIght (detail)
materials: Linen & Silk
size: 7m x 2.5m x 1.5m

title: Field (detail)
materials: Linen, Silk & Bamboo
size: 3.05m x 3.05m

BIOGRAPHY ASAKO ISHIZAKI

Selected Exhibitions

1989	ITF International Textile Competition, Kyoto,Japan
1992	Biennale International de Lausanne,
	Musee Cantonnal des Beaux Arts, Lausanne, Switzerland
1996	1ere Biennale Du LIN Haute Normandie, France
1997	5th ITF International Textile Competition, Kyoto, Japan
	Textile Art From Kyoto, Sweden
1999	Our Most Beautiful Embroidered Stories, France
	6th ITF International Textile Competition, Kyoto, Japan
1999	2eme Biennale Du LIN Contemporain, France

石崎 朝子

harumi ISOBE

a woven text naming extinct and endangered flora

作品に織り込まれている文字は、絶滅植物と絶滅の危険がある植物の名称です。

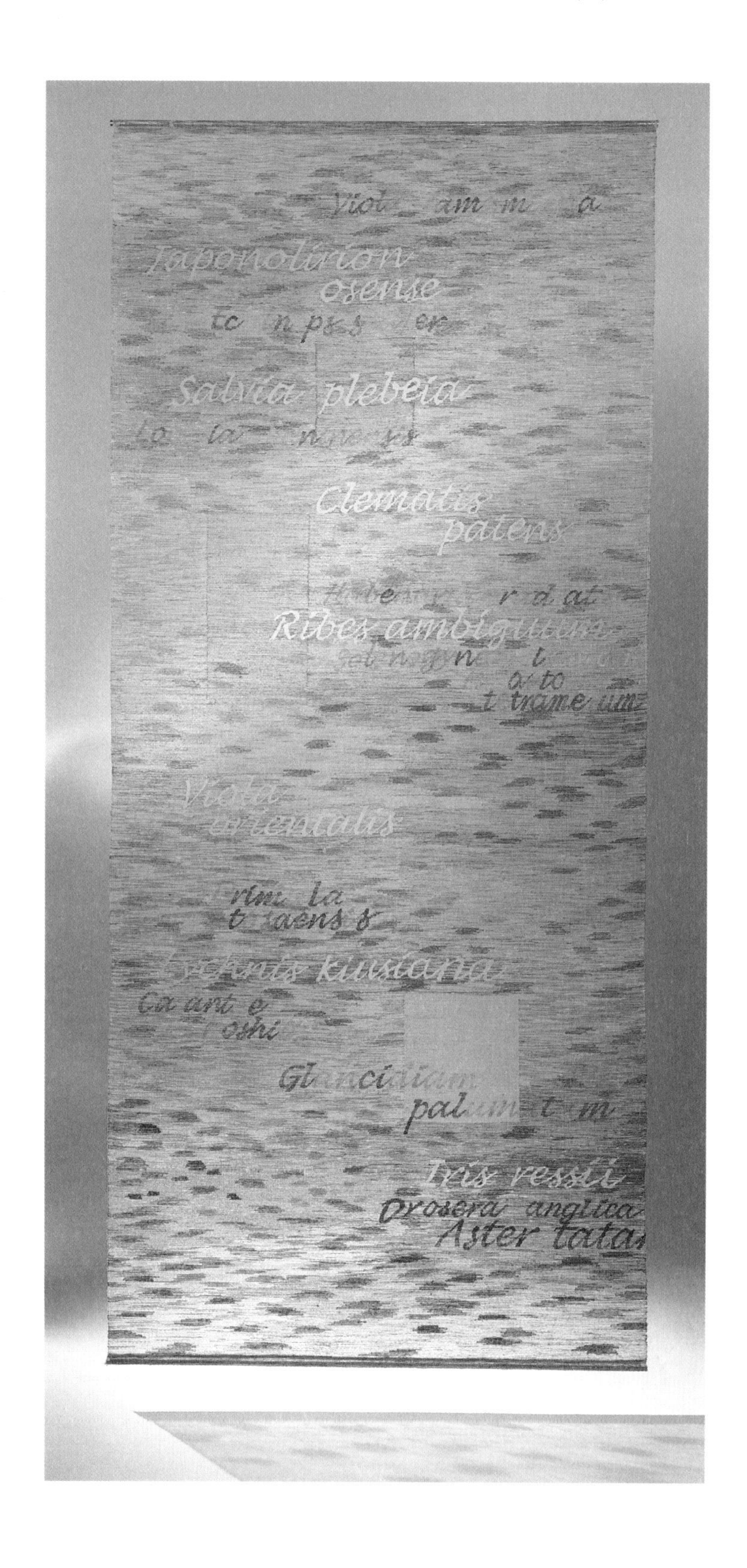

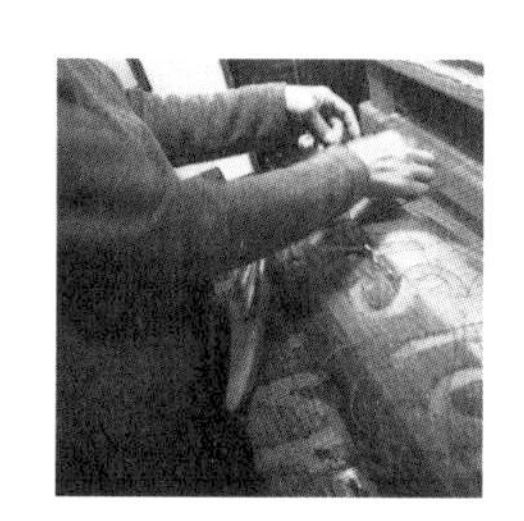

title: Missa Flora 2
materials: Linen & silk
size: 3.50m x l.57m

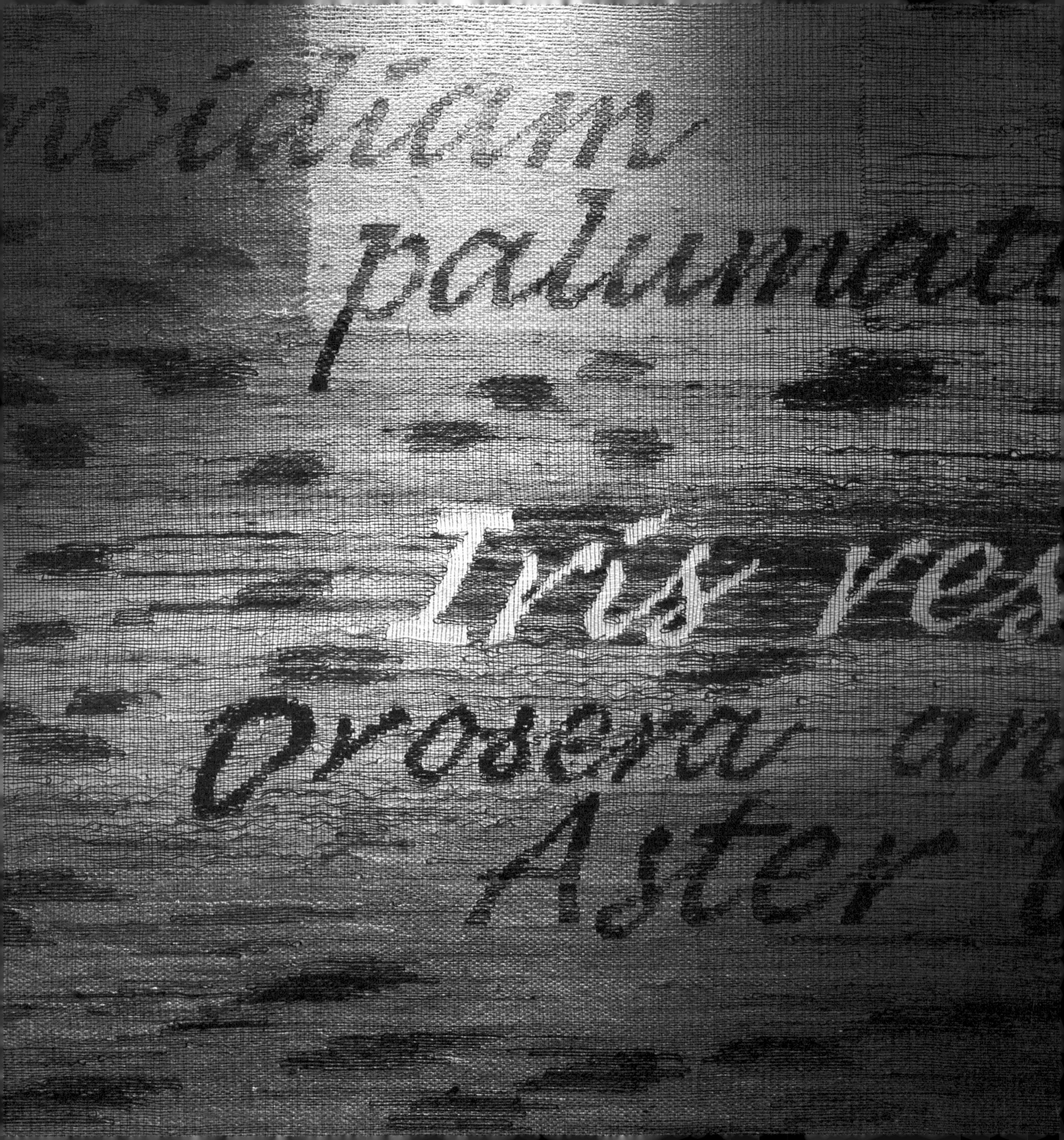

ncianam
palumnat
Tris res
Drosera an
Aster

pleated pieces conceal almost as much as they reveal

ひだで隠れている部分は表面に現れている部分とほぼ同じです。

■ After working as a textile designer for a fabric company, Harumi Isobe trained in Sweden to be a tapestry weaver. Tapestry is a relatively new medium for textile artists in Japan and her approach is one in which three dimensional qualities are very important. These are achieved in several ways: through texture and colour, by folding and pleating, by layering one piece in front of another or by transparency. The pleated pieces conceal almost as much as they reveal, the tapestry is woven at least one third wider than the finished piece then, once off the loom, it is gathered in at certain points, hiding the woven surface within its folds.

Isobe lived in England for many years and her works contain elements which reflect the differing approaches of East and West. Her work refers directly to particular concepts which are those traditional ones of nature, harmony and beauty that lie at the centre of all the artists work in the exhibition. However Isobe views these elements in a specific and focussed way. This demonstrates her position of influences from both cultures - the conceptual approach behind her work has the Western concern with content but the means employed to express these concerns are texture, structure and light. The use of the gathering and 'shrinking' of 'Earth Cardiogram' illustrates the sensation that the earth is becoming smaller and more vulnerable, the colours of the work drawn from the shadow, the darkness. The pleats and the movement of colour are indications of fissures in the earth's crust and also relate to cardiogram printouts.

■ 磯部晴美は、テキスタイルデザイナーとして繊維会社に勤務した後、スウェーデンでタペストリーの織り手として研鑽を積みました。日本の織物アーティストにとって、タペストリーは比較的新しい表現手段です。磯部のアプローチでは、立体感がとても重要ですが、この立体感を出すには、次のようないくつかの方法があります。すなわち、織物と色彩、折り曲げてひだを作る、作品を他の作品に重ねる、透明感を醸し出すことです。ひだで隠れている部分と表面に現れている部分とほぼ同じです。タペストリーは、少なくとも最終作品よりも3倍の大きさに織ります。機織り機から外した後、数箇所でまとめ、織った表面を折り目の中に隠します。

磯部はイングランドに何年間も住んでおり、その作品には東洋と西洋の異なるアプローチの要素が表れています。その作品は、自然、調和、美の伝統的な概念を直接表現しています。これらの概念は、展示会の芸術家全員の中心概念でもありますが、磯部はこれらの要素を具体的に絞り込んで考え、双方の文化の影響を表現しています。その作品の根本にある概念的アプローチは、内容を考える西洋の発想ですが、これらを表現する手段は、織物、構造、光なのです。「Earth Cardiogram」では、ひだと「縮み」を活かし、大地(Earth)が小さく、弱くなっていくという感覚を表現しています。その色彩で影や闇を描いています。ひだや色彩の動きは大地の地殻の亀裂を表し、心電図(Cardiogram)でもあります。

title: Earth Cardiogram
materials: Wool, Linen, Cotton & Lurex
size: 1.7m x 2.5m

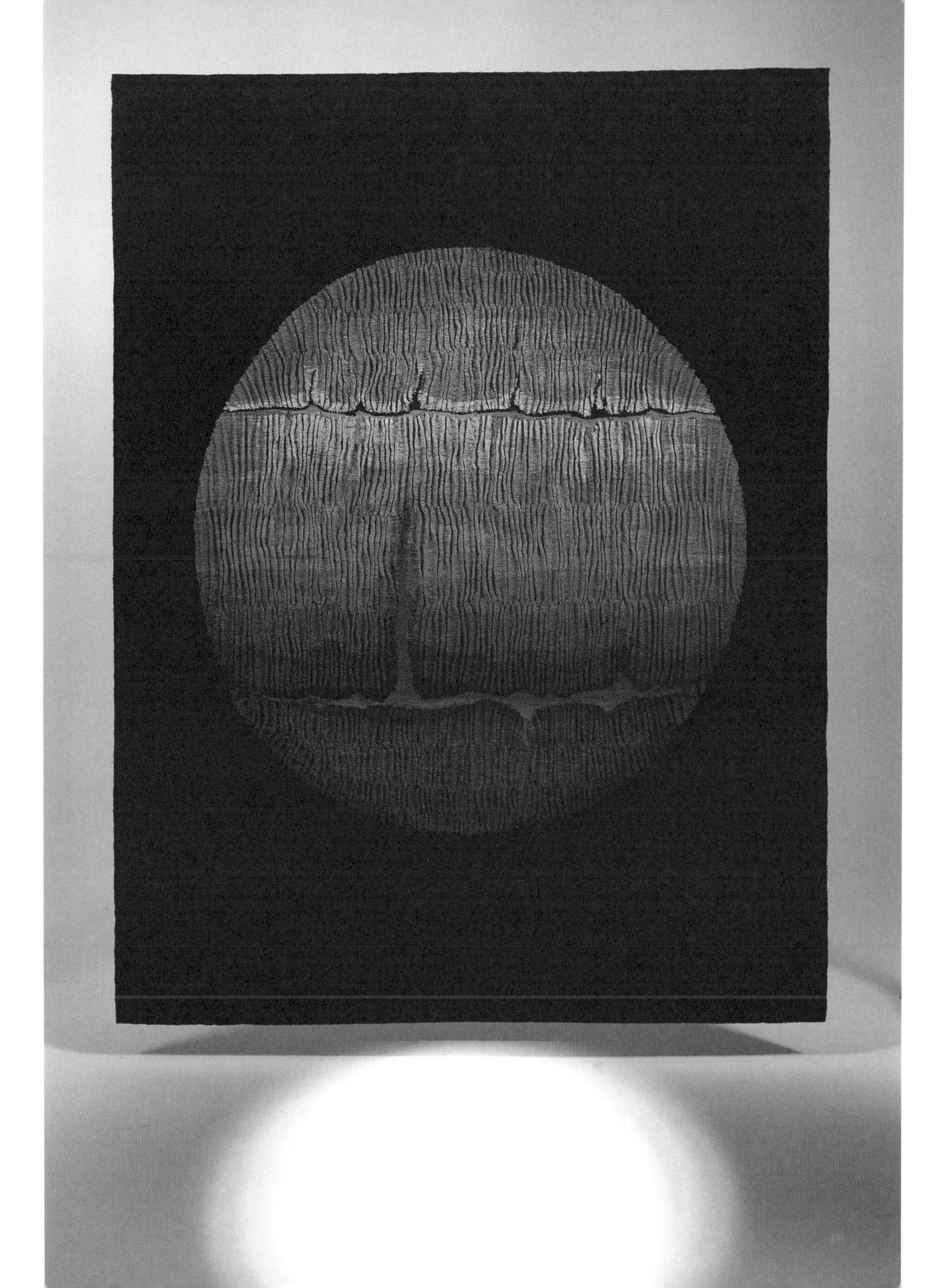

Isobe's use of light and colour draws on a wide range of experience of European artists, linking these to the acute aesthetic judgements of Japanese craft traditions. The delicate colours and the transparent, fragile nature of the inlay tapestries 'Missa Flora 1 & 2' echo her view of the transient nature of existence, the text woven within the pieces naming extinct and endangered flora. As we look through the tapestry our view of its surrounding space is tempered by the textures and text within the work. These transparent works are light and ethereal in their revelation allowing the light through whereas the pleated works are extremely heavy in their concealment absorbing and reflecting the light.

磯部は光と色彩を活かしていますが、これは欧州の芸術家達の幅広い経験も活用しています。これらを日本の伝統的な工芸における鋭い審美眼と結びつけているのです。微妙な色彩、透明さ、繊細さを散りばめられたタペストリー、「Missa Flora　1&2」は、存在がはかないものであるとする磯部の考え方を投影しています。作品に織り込まれている文字は、絶滅植物と絶滅の危険がある植物の名称です。見ている者は作品の周りの空間を見ながら、周りの空間と、タペストリーの織地や文字とを調和させるのです。これらの透明な作品群では光が通り抜け、空気のように軽やかな優美さを啓示しています。その一方で、ひだのある作品群では光を反射させ、また光を吸収して閉じ込めており、非常に重い作品となっています。

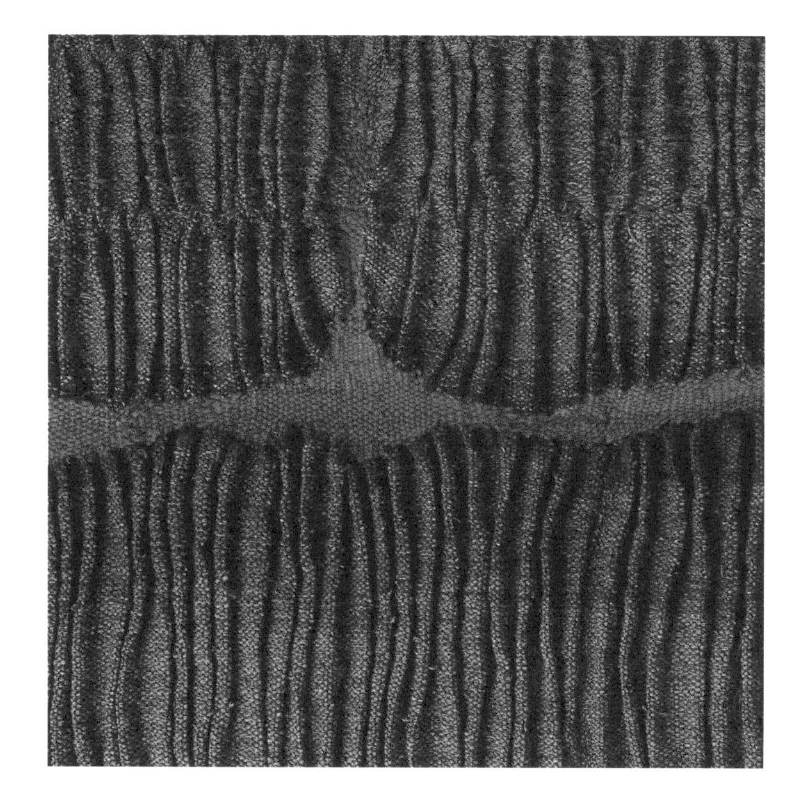

title: Earth Cardiogram (detail)
materials: Wool, Linen, Cotton & Lurex
size: 1.7m x 2.5m

BIOGRAPHY HARUMI ISOBE

Selected Exhibitions

1976	Fibre Works Europe/Japan
	National Museum of Modern Art Kyoto & Tokyo
1983	Textile Exhibition, Museum of Modern Art, Gunma
1992/93	International Tapestry Network Exhibition, Travelling U.S.A.
1992/95/98	Solo Exhibition, Gallery Maronie, Kyoto & Gallery Senbikiya,Tokyo
1996	Revelation, Touring UK.
1997	Textile Art From Kyoto, Gallery M, Stockholm, Sweden
1998	Revelation, National Museum of Modern Art, Kyoto
	Revelation Miniatures, Gallery Gallery Kyoto
	Itami Museum of Art and Craft, Hyogo
1999	Solo Exhibition, Itami Museum of Art and Craft, Hyogo
	Solo Exhibition, Daiwa Foundation, London
2000	Woven Garden, Tapestry Exhibition, Belgium

磯辺 晴美

studio KOBAYASHI

relationship with surroundings is fundamental to their work

環境との関連性を表現することが、2人の作品の基本です。

The Kobayashis live in the mountains outside Kyoto in a house containing their living area and workspace. It was built by Masakazu and reflects their feeling for and about space, light and harmony, embodying, through its design, concepts of particularity and universality. Their relationship to and with their surroundings is fundamental to their work. Naomi Kobayashi talks of the countryside around the house making her deeply conscious of 'the cycles of nature and my own place in the universe. The intention of my recent works, then, is to communicate the unity of the never-ending providence of nature; the cycle of life; the eternal cycles of the universe.'

Both Kobayashis are established and acclaimed artists in their own right, more recently they have chosen to exhibit together, giving joint expression to their common philosophy. However the work is still created separately and then brought together as a conscious, collaborative act. Their installation for the exhibition contains several distinct but related units. Masakazu Kobayashi's 'Gate of Bow' and 'Pond of Bow' are the first elements we encounter. They are made up of many tensile 'bows' which are created by coiling thread on a fine aluminium shaft.

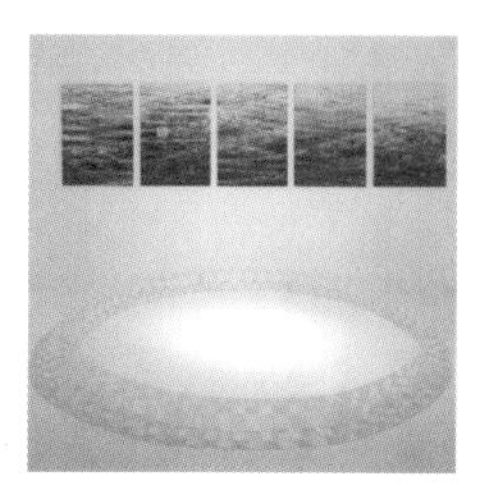

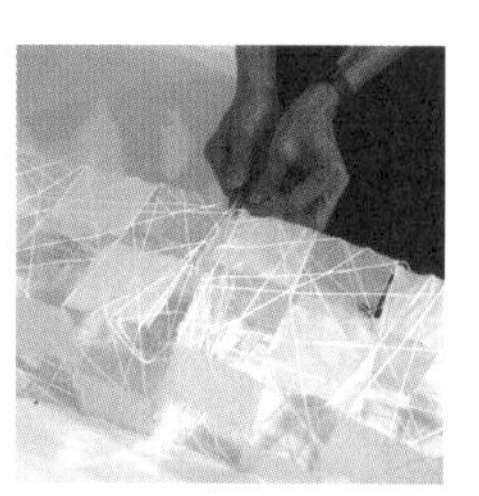

title: Work 98 #105 (detail)
materials: Cotton & Paper
size: Room installation (Wall)

1

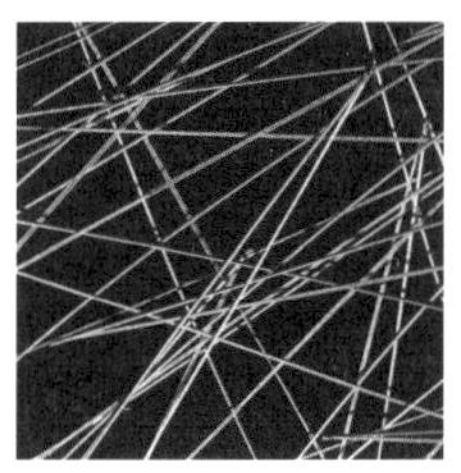

2

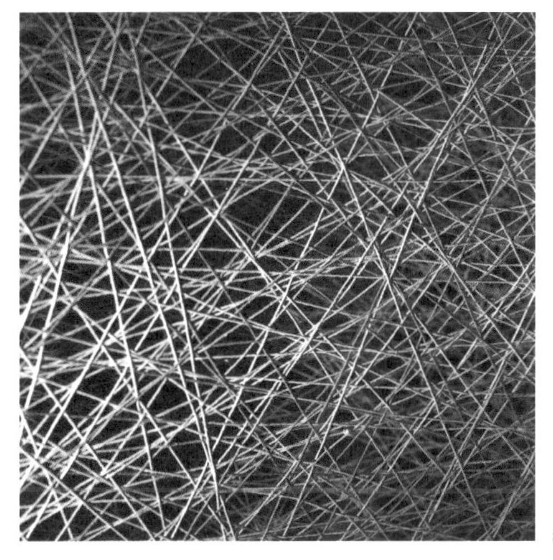

3

■ 小林夫婦は京都郊外の山中に住み、創作もここで行っています。家は正和が建築したもので、そのデザインは個別性と普遍性の双方の概念を具現化しており、空間、光、調和に対する2人の心が表れています。環境との関連性を表現することが、2人の作品の基本です。小林尚美は、「山中の環境で、自然の循環と宇宙における自分の立場を深く意識します。最近の作品の目的は、終わることのない自然の摂理の調和、すなわち、生命の輪、宇宙の永遠の輪を伝えることです。」と語っています。

小林夫婦は2人別々に芸術家としての地位を確立し、賞賛されてきました。最近になって一緒に展示会を開くことにし、共通の哲学を共同で表現しています。しかし、今も作品は別々に創作し、協力の賜物として1つにまとめています。この2人の出展作品には、異なってはいるものの互いに関連性のある作品がいくつかあります。展示では、小林正和の「Gate of Bow」と「Pond of Bow」がまず目に入ります。この作品は、精巧なアルミニウムの軸に糸を巻きつけて弾力性のある弓（bow）を作成し、その弓を数多く合わせて創作しています。これらの弓を慎重に無作為に配分することにより、作品の中心テーマである秩序と混乱の微妙なバランスを表しているのです。正和は、1本の糸に備わっている可能性と線の重要性に言及しています。これらの2つの作品を見ると、1本の線が無限に組み合わさった結果であることに気づきます。それぞれの糸が空間の動きを決定し、隣接する糸と糸との関係を設定し、その関係により作品が決定されています。弓にはそれぞれ進む方向がありますが、皆非常に短いために、弓を追う視線の歩みはすぐに止まり、常に作品全体の影響を考えることになります。そのために、リニア（線）構造の深さにますます気づくのです。

title: Installation (previous page) – front - Gate of Bow[3], Pond of Bow[2], middle - Ma 2000, wall - Work 98 #105
materials: Aluminium & Silk, Paper & Paper thread, Cotton & Paper
size: Room installation

an intention to draw on the cycles of life, death and regeneration

生命、死、再生という永遠の輪を描こうとしています。

The distribution of these bows is deliberately random within the parameters of the piece reflecting the delicate balance between order and chaos which is central to the work. Masakazu refers to the importance of line and the possibilities inherent in the single thread, as we look at these two works we are aware of the effect of an accumulation of many, many single lines. Each thread determines a movement in space and each is dependant upon and sets up a relationship with its neighbour. Each bow creates a sense of its own direction but because each is quite short, the travel of the eye is halted, continuously returning to the impact of the totality of the piece, increasingly aware of the density of the linear structure.

Beyond these dense and overlaid structures of Masakazu Kobayashi we look to Naomi Kobayashi's white circle. Made from twisted paper thread and Washi (Japanese paper) it creates a sense of weightlessness. The circle both contains light and allows light to pass through, seeming to generate a luminous surface encompassing the many colours of white. Where Masakazu's work gives the appearance of random movement, Naomi's circle creates a sense of stillness. Underlying this there is an intention to draw on the eternal cycles of life, death and regeneration inherent in the basic form of the circle, creating an equilibrium with its surroundings. The threads which hold the circle together are intended to be symbolic of the link between the cosmos and our everyday life.

小林正和が創作したこれらの深い重層構造の向こうに、小林尚美の白い輪が見えます。尚美の作品では、和紙と和紙の「こより」から軽い感触が生まれています。輪は光を含みつつも光を透過させており、多くの白系の色彩を含んだ光沢のある表面になっているように見えます。小林正和の作品が無作為に動いているように見えるのに対し、 尚美の輪は静止の感覚を創生し、このもとで、生命、死、再生という永遠の輪を描こうとしています。これらは輪の基本形であり、環境と均衡を保っています。これらの輪をつなぐ糸は、宇宙と日常生活のつながりを象徴しています。

展示会では、次に景観を構成する小林尚美の織物5作品が続きます。この作品では、自分で描いた絵画を細片に破り、それらを縫っています。縫うという行為により、かすかに動くイメージが醸しだされ、この5作品に波打つような流れを与えています。立体を吊り下げているために、床にある輪から壁にかかっている織物へと、視点が移っていきます。

title: Kaku 2000 No. 101, 102, 103
materials: Cotton, Handmade Paper & Perspex
size: each 0.46m x 0.36m x 0.05m

title: Ito Kukan
materials: Paper & Cotton
size: each 0.80m x 0.75m x 0.15m

The installation continues with five woven pieces by Naomi Kobayashi which together form a landscape. Made from paintings by her which have been torn into strips and woven, the act of weaving causing the image to move slightly giving the undulating flow across the five works. The suspended cube form carries the visual impetus from the floor based circle to the wall based weavings.

Naomi Kobayashi has two other works in the exhibition. 'Kaku 2000' is made up of 3 works in Perspex boxes. These pieces are woven from the many calligraphic Buddhist texts written by her mother on handmade paper which Kobayashi has recycled and spun into threads. The work is displayed to deliberately allow the viewer to see both sides – the flat and the textured, the concealed and the revealed. 'Ito Kukan' consists of 2 white boxes whose volume is created through light and shadow. In the circle piece the light is allowed to pass through whereas in 'Ito Kukan' the paper absorbs and reflects the light. It is essential that the angle of the work in relation to the wall is seen in such a way that the cast shadow forms a distinct indicator of the illusory three dimensional nature of the work. The substance and the shadow, the positive and the negative, what is there and what is not there.

小林尚美は、他にも2つの作品を展示しています。「Kaku 2000」は、パースペックス（アクリル）ボックスの3作品で構成されています。これらの作品は、尚美の母が書いた経文を多く織り込んでいます。経文は和紙に書いたもので、小林がそれを糸に紡いだのです。作品には慎重な工夫が施され、織物の両側を見られます。裏側と表側、隠されている側と表出されている側の双方です。「Ito Kukan」は2つの白いボックスで構成され、その大きさは光と影で創生されています。輪の作品では光は透過できましたが、「Ito Kukan」では、和紙は光を吸収して反射します。壁に対する作品の角度は、壁に投影された影が、作品の幻想的な立体性を鮮やかに映し出すようになっています。実体とその影、正と負、存在と無が表現されています。

BIOGRAPHY MASAKAZU KOBAYASHI

Selected Exhibitions

1973/75/77/79	Biennale International de Lausanne Musee Cantonal des Beaux-Arts, Lausanne, Switzerland
1975/78	International Textile Triennale, Lodz, Poland
1987/92/95/99	International Textile Competition, Kyoto, Japan
1991	Restless Shadows, Goldsmiths Gallery London, & touring UK.
1993	Crafts Of the World, National Museum of Modern Art, Kyoto, Japan
1994	Japanese Design, Philadelphia Museum of Art, U.S.A.
1995	Japanese Studio Crafts, Victoria and Albert Museum, London, UK.

Awards

1975	Prize, Ministry of Culture and Art 2nd Textile Triennale, Lodz, Poland
1978	Prize 1st Enba Exhibition The National Museum of Modern Art, Kyoto, Japan
1991	New Artist Award 1st Takashimaya Culture foundation, Japan
1994	Excellence Award 4th International Textile Competition, Kyoto, Japan
1996	Gold Medal 6th Kyoto Arts Festival, Japan

Collections

The National Museum of Modern Art, Kyoto, Japan, Philadelphia Museum of Art, U.S.A., The National Museum of Art, Osaka, Japan, Kyoto City Museum, Japan, Victoria and Albert Museum, London, UK.

BIOGRAPHY NAOMI KOBAYASHI

Selected Exhibitions

1976/78/80	International Miniature Textile, London, UK.
1977/79/85/89/92	Biennale International de Lausanne, Musee Cantonal des Beaux-Arts, Lausanne, Switzerland
1978/81	International Textile Triennale, Lodz, Poland
1991	Restless Shadows, Goldsmiths Gallery London, & touring UK.
1992	SANAT '92 Earth and Fibre Exhibition, Ankara, Turkey
1989/94/99	International Textile Competition, Kyoto, Japan
1995	16th Lausanne Biennale 'Criss-Crossing' Lausanne, Musee Cantonal des Beaux-Arts, Lausanne, Switzerland
1998	Structure and Surface - Contemporary Japanese Textile, Museum of Modern Art, New York & touring U.S.A.

Awards

1981	Gold Medal 4th International Textile Triennale, Lodz, Poland
1989	Outsider Award International Textile Competition, Kyoto, Japan

Collections

Central Museum of Textiles, Lodz, Poland, Stedelijk Museum, Amsterdam, Holland, Museum Bellerive, Zurich, Switzerland, American Craft Museum New York, U.S.A., St. Louis Art Museum, Missouri U.S.A., Victoria and Albert Museum, London, UK., Israel Museum, Metropolitan Museum, New York, U.S.A.

小林正和

小林尚美

shigeo KUBOTA

to make visible that which is invisible

見えないものを目で見えるように表現する。

The idea of contradiction, of opposites, which eventually come together as a harmonious whole, is the basis of Shigeo Kubota's work. Using the humblest materials, sisal hemp for the weft and ramie as the warp, and the most basic technique, plain weave, the long thin woven strips are sewn together to create the most complex three-dimensional structures. His palette is also simple, red and green, black and white, occasionally blue and yellow, the colours indicating the tension of opposites which are contained in the form. Born into a family of traditional weavers, the integrity of his approach is demonstrated by his belief that the structure of the woven cloth is the most important factor in realising the finished work. It is that dichotomy between the fundamental process of weaving and the complexity of the sewn structure which governs the outcome.

矛盾と対置の発想は、全体の中に調和してまとまります。これが久保田繁雄の作品の基本です。緯糸にサイザル麻、経糸にラミーという最も素朴な素材を、そして平織りという最も基本的な技術を使用して長くて薄い布を織り、それを縫い合わせて最も複雑で立体的な構造を創り出しています。色彩もまたシンプルです。赤、緑、黒、白、時には黄色という色彩様式が、相反するものを表し、緊張感を醸し出しています。機織りの家系に生まれた久保田氏のアプローチは完璧です。この完璧さは作品を完成させるために、織り布の構造が最も重要な要因であるとの信念の賜物です。織るという基本的な作業と、織い上げた織り布の構造の複雑は対照的です。そして、この構造が作品を決定しています。

title: Woven Corridor – From Italy
materials: Gold Thread & Sisal
size: No.1- 2.11m high, No.2 - 1.92m high, No.3 - 1.76m high

Space, light and shadow are immediately apparent as important elements in the work, the sisal hemp having particular light reflecting qualities. Here again are ideas of paradox, the wish to make visible that which is invisible (space), the shadow being as important within the work as the light. The sounds and rhythms of nature have been starting points as he has searched to give material form to these intangibles. 'Echo of the Wind No. X' has a particular history, Kubota usually works on a cloth loom but for this piece he built a frame loom and used a tightly spun sisal yarn. Using the movement of the warp as he worked, he allowed the process and the materials to influence the outcome, exploiting the richness and diversity residing in what he refers to as 'the language of yarn'.

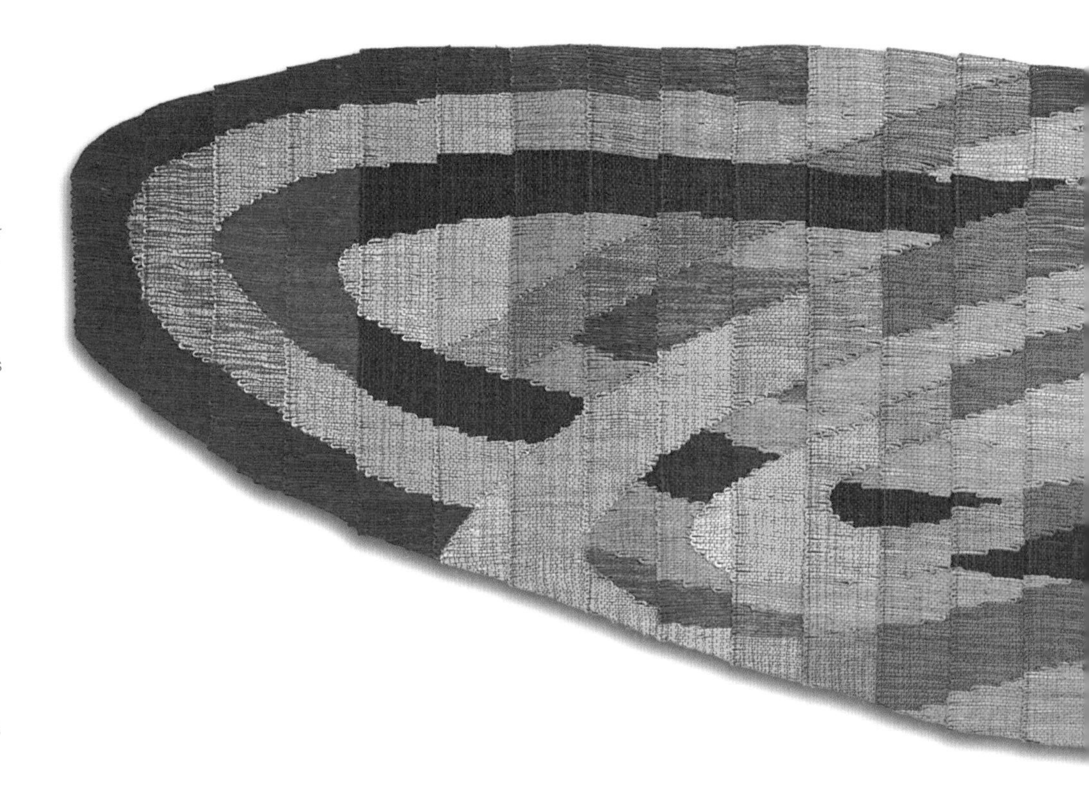

The floor standing installation in the exhibition 'Woven Corridor - From Italy' marks a new phase in his work. In 1999 Kubota spent some time in Italy and was very impressed by the architecture of the many churches and cathedrals he visited, and the specific dynamic structure of the buildings. The particular geometry and perspective, the rich colours and the innate spirituality within these places of worship have inspired this work. The gold warp brings together the two cultures, not only referring to the interior of the churches but also it is another use of light, the light within and the light which is drawn from the shadows.

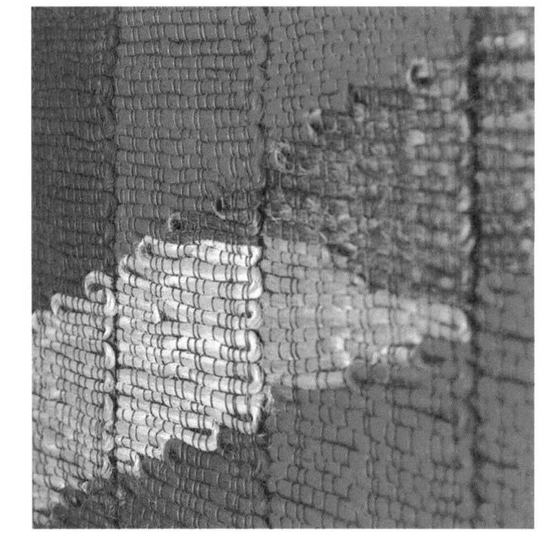

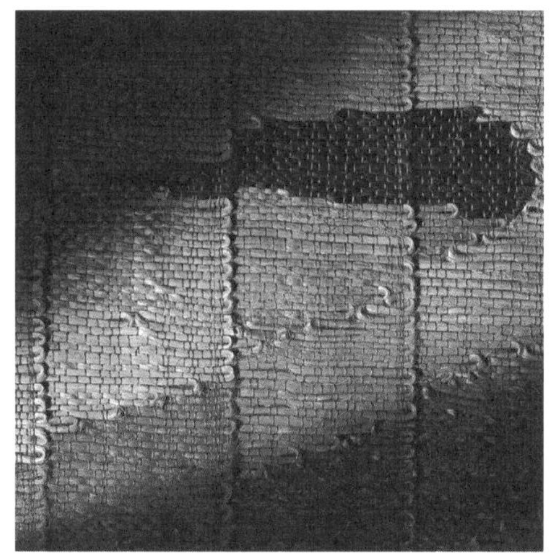

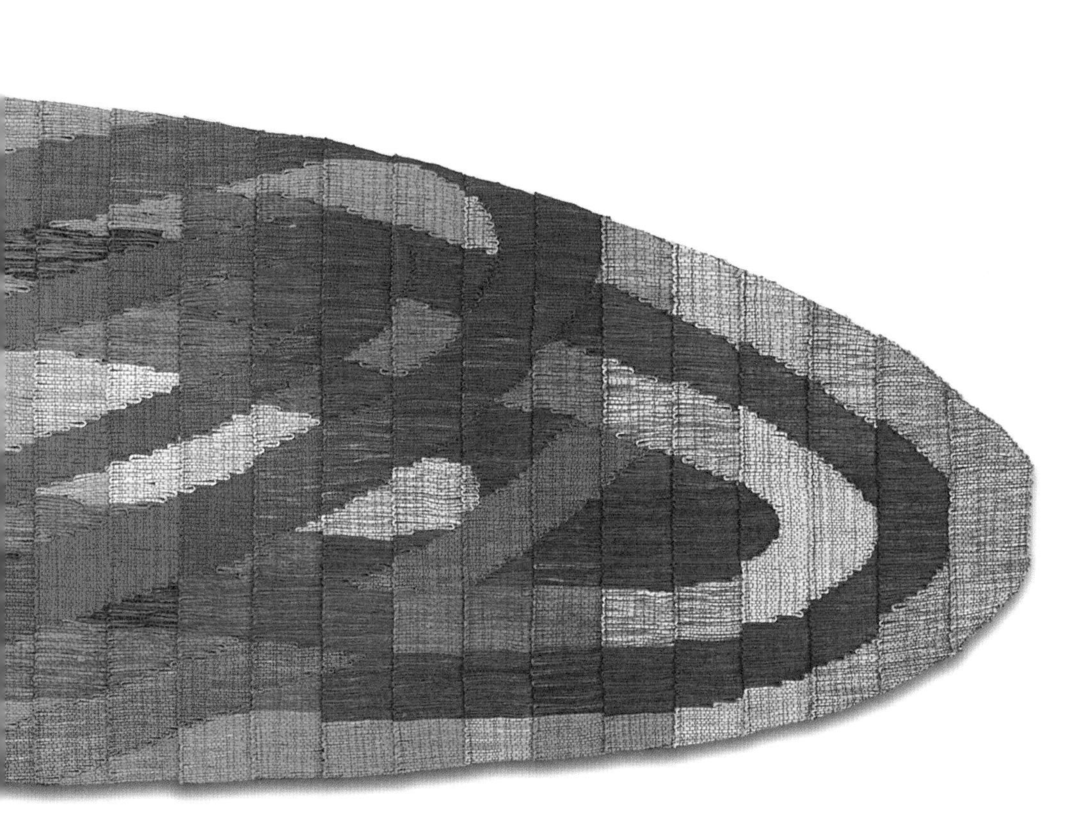

空間、光、影は、作品の重要な構成要素で、目で見てすぐにわかります。特に、サイザル麻は光を反射する特性があります。ここでまた、矛盾の発想が登場します。見えないもの(空間)を目で見えるように表現したいという望みがあるために、影が光同様に作品において重要な役割を果たします。見えないものや触れることができないものに、具体的な形を与えようと模索した際に、まず自然の音とリズムから始めました。「Echo of the Wind No.X」の創作工程は独特です。久保田は通常、布の機織り機で作業しますが、この作品では、フレーム織り機できつく紡いだサイザル糸を使用し、経糸の動きをうまく使いながら作成しました。その際、その工程と素材が作品の結果に影響を与えています。「織り糸の言葉」と同氏が表現する多様性と細工の細かさが活かされているのです。

床に建てられている展示物、「Woven Corridor-From Italy」は、作品が新しい段階に入ったことを示しています。1999年に久保田はイタリアで過ごして多くの教会や大聖堂を訪れ、その建築のダイナミックな構築や構造に感銘を受けています。これらの崇拝の場における豊かな色彩、特有の霊的雰囲気、独特の構造や視点が、この作品のひらめきとなりました。金色の経糸は2つの文化を縫い合わせています。教会内部だけでなく、光をも表しています。それは、影から導き出される光です。

title: Echo Of The Wind 10
materials: Sisal Hemp & Ramie
size: 1.5m x 4.7m

exploiting the richness and diversity residing in 'the language of yarn'

「織り糸の言葉」と久保田が表現する多様性と細工の細かさが活かされている。

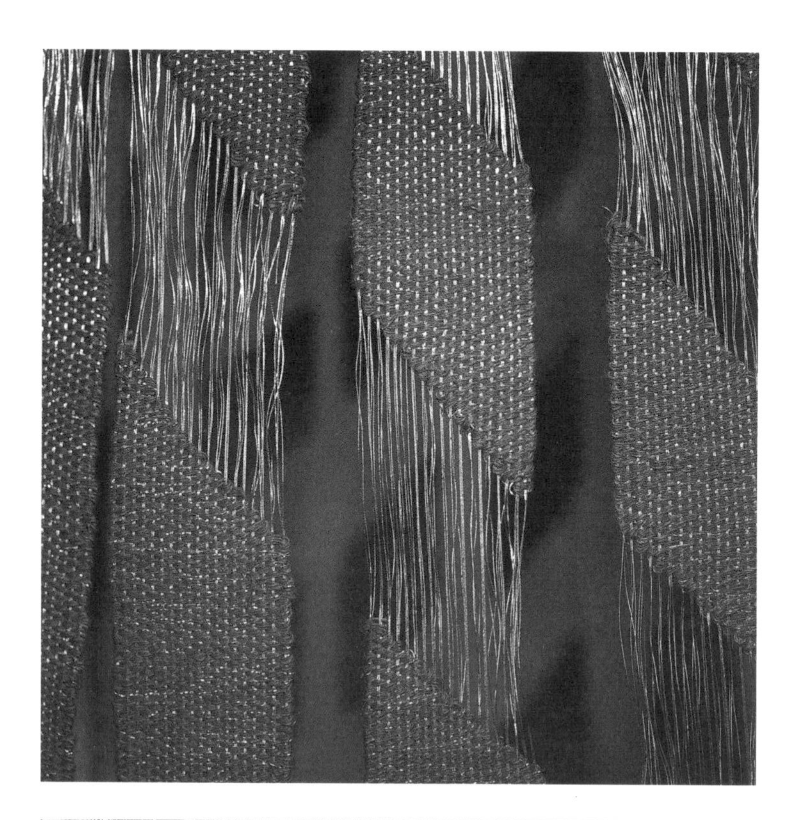

title: Woven Corridor – From Italy (detail)
materials: Gold Thread & Sisal
size: No.1- 2.11m high, No.2- 1.92m high, No.3- 1.76m high

BIOGRAPHY SHIGEO KUBOTA

Exhibitions Include

1975/77/83/87/89	Biennale International de Lausanne Musee Cantonal des Beaux-Arts, Lausanne, Switzerland
1978	3rd International Textile Triennale, Lodz, Poland
1984-85	Contemporary Japanese Fibre Works, Museum Belle Rive, Zurich, Switzerland, Textile Museum Tilburg, Holland, Museum of Decorative Art, Lausanne, Switzerland
1989	Japanese Fibre Work, Gallery of Western Australia, Perth, Australia
1993	Modern Japanese Textile Arts, Beauty of Material and Skill, Fukushima Museum of Art, Japan
1995	Contemporary Japanese Craft, Tradition and Avant Garde, Victoria and Albert Museum, London UK
1995/96/98	Osaka Triennale, Japan
1999	The 20th-Century Textile Artist, The Art Institute of Chicago, USA The Genealogy of Craft Objects, The National Museum of Modern Art, Tokyo, Japan

Prizes and Public Collections

1983/4	Research of Fibre Art in U.S.A., Fellowship from The Agency for Cultural Affairs, Overseas Art Programme
1985	The New Talent Prize, Kyoto Municipality
1986	38th Kyoto Art Exhibition Supreme Prize
1996	Osaka Triennale 1996-Painting, Special prize
1997	Study and solo exhibition in Edinburgh under Artist-in Residence scheme, Art-Ex.
1998	International Art Exhibition Tenri Biennale Grand Prix

久保田 繁雄

kyoko KUMAI

an impression of floating movement, a sense of weightlessness

軽い感覚と浮遊の印象

Kyoko Kumai's fluid steel lines attempt to follow the tracks of the wind, holding the movement of the moment, seemingly in a state of transience. Although there is monumentality in her works, they are also the antithesis of what we expect from this material. The quality of light, both reflected and within the work, adds to the impression of floating movement, the sense of weightlessness.

熊井恭子の流動鋼線は風が吹き去った跡を追い、一過性の状態、一瞬の動きを捉えます。作品のスケールは雄大ですが、この作品はこの素材から連想される印象へのアンチテーゼでもあります。光は、反射される光、吸い込まれる光ともに、軽い感覚と浮遊の印象を与えます。

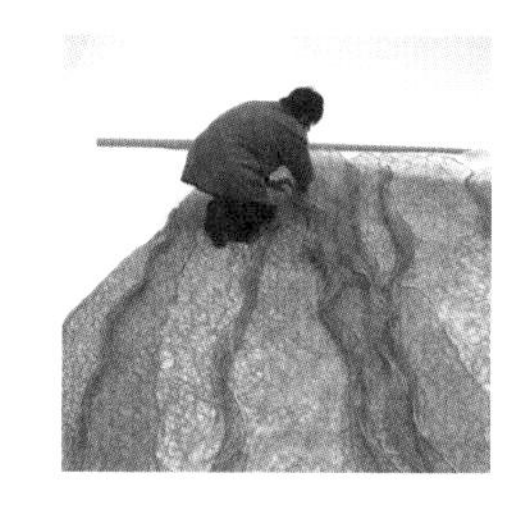

title: Wind From the Cloud
materials: Stainless Steel
size: 3m x 2m

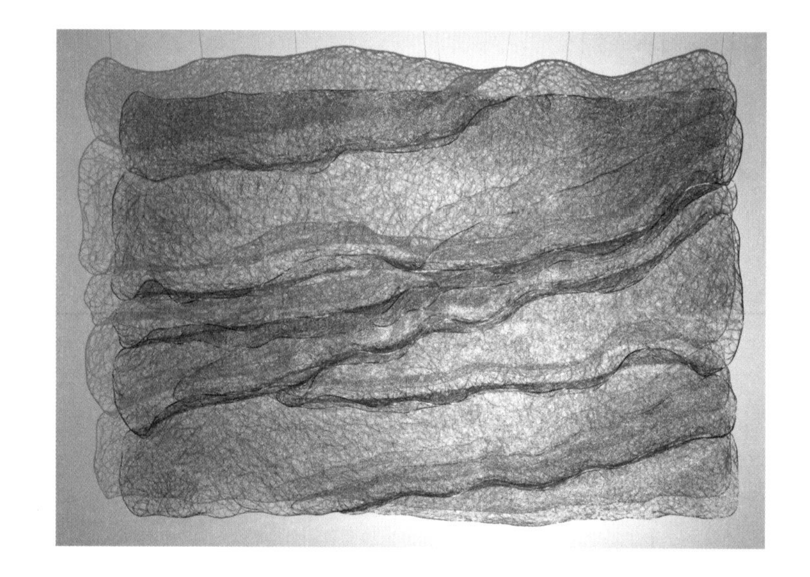

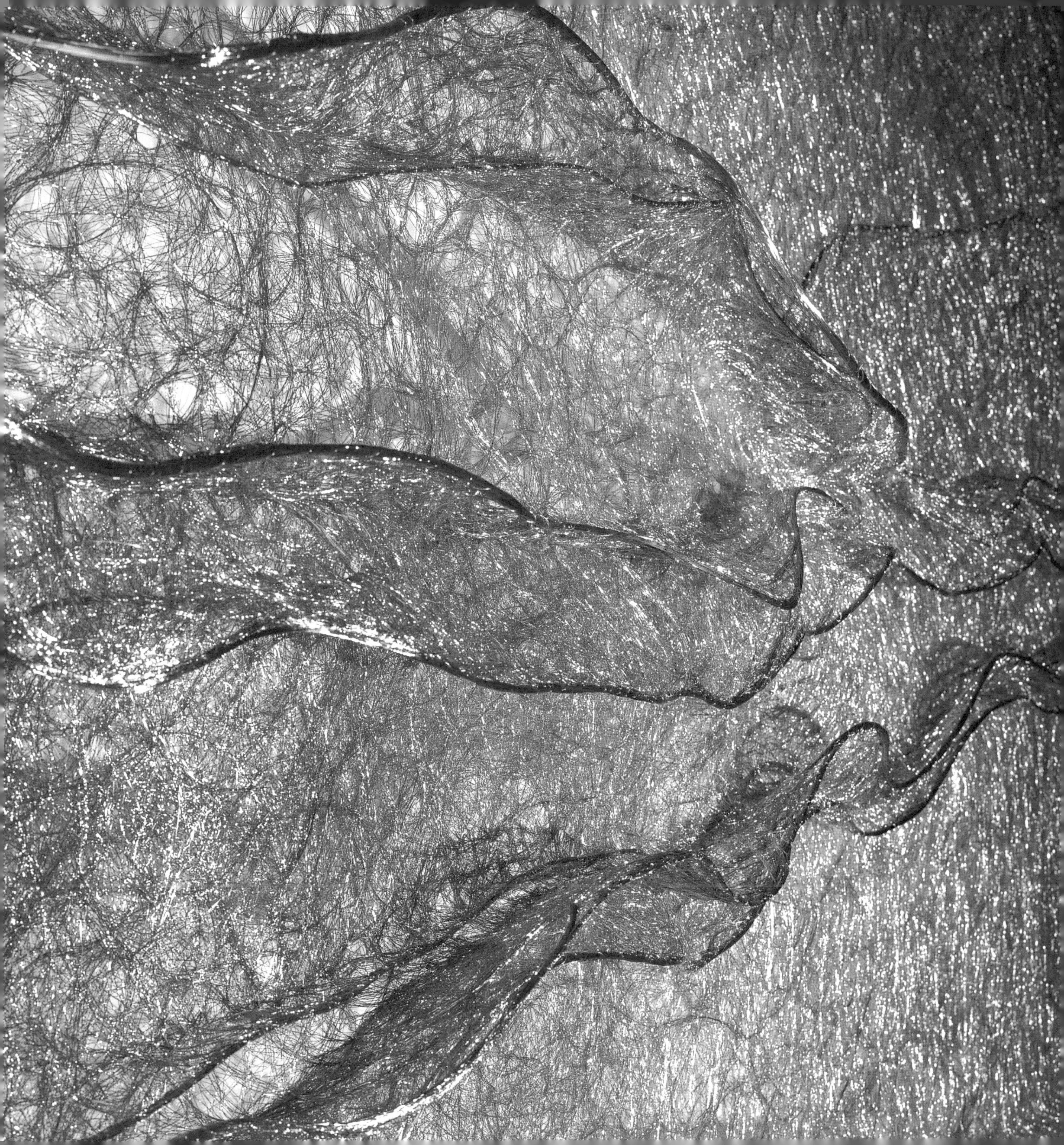

describing invisible currents of air billowing and folding

うねって巻きつく空気の流れ、見えないはずの空気の流れ

Initially Kumai worked as a weaver, gradually developing her own interlacing and knotting techniques as a response to the steel and she has been working with this material for over 20 years. Kumai is much concerned that her works 'express the cycles of life' and connect the organic and inorganic through the processes of making. There is the sense that the steel is used as much for its inherent possibilities in interpreting her ideas about the natural world as for the unspoken contradiction in using an industrial material to echo an elemental force of nature. 'Wind From The Cloud' is a wall mounted work created by an interlacing technique using stainless steel filaments. The materials are placed at random on the floor then intertwined using a shuttle or needle. The resulting fabric seems, in turn, solid or transparent depending on our position in relation to the work. The light source is of particular importance to this piece and as different intensities of light play across it, the work can appear to be either a series of fissures or to be describing invisible currents of air, billowing and folding.

Kumai's continuing inspiration for her work has been the movement of air, in particular the wind moving through grass, in which she revisits early childhood memories. The illusion of this phenomenon is created in 'Grass' and is reinstated each time it is seen. For the purposes of transportation the work is rolled, flattening the 'blades' of steel, meaning that each knotted strand must be carefully re-positioned for every installation, re-creating that specific movement in time. Kumai's intention is that the stainless steel becomes the wind and contains the air.

もともと熊井は織り職人でした。徐々に鋼鉄を織り交ぜて結ぶ独自の技術を開発し、今では20年間以上もこの素材を作品で扱っています。熊井は、作品が「生命の循環を表現する」ことと、制作の際に有機質と無機質をつなぐことに非常に気を使っています。自然界に対する考えを表す際は、鋼鉄を使用します。工業的な素材を使用して暗黙の矛盾を表します。こうして、自然の壮大な力を反映させるのです。ここに鋼鉄独自の可能性があると考えています。「Wind From The Cloud」は、ステンレス鋼フィラメントを織り混ぜる技術を使用して創作し、壁に固定した作品です。素材は床の上に無作為に置き、織り機のシャットルか針で相互に巻きつけます。その結果、見る位置により織物が時にはどっしりと、時には透明に見えます。この作品では、光の源が特に重要です。作品に様々な光の強さが射すと、裂け目の連続か、うねって巻きつく空気の流れ、見えないはずの空気の流れが見えてきます。

熊井の作品の絶えざるひらめきのもとは、空気の動きです。特に、風が草原を吹き抜ける幼い頃の思い出を、熊井はよく思い出しています。この幻想の様子は、「Grass」で創造されています。この作品を見るたびに、当時が再現されるのです。この作品は搬送するために、巻いて鋼鉄の「刃」は平らにしています。つまり、展示のたびに、結んだ線を慎重に再度設置し、当時の動きを再現します。熊井はステンレス鋼を空気と風にしようとしているのです。

title: Grass
materials: Stainless Steel
size: 4m x 5m

title: Grass (detail)
materials: Stainless Steel
size: 4m x 5m

BIOGRAPHY KYOKO KUMAI

Selected Exhibitions

1987 Biennale International de Lausanne Musee Cantonal des Beaux-Arts, Lausanne)

1st International Textile Competition Kyoto. New Technology Prize

1991 Solo exhibition Museum of Modern Art, New York.

1994 Textile and New Technology, Crafts Council London

1995 Japanese Studio Crafts, Victoria and Albert Museum, London

1997 Challenge of Materials, Science Museum, London

1998 International Tapestry Triennale, Lodz. Bronze Prize

1999 Contemporary Arts of Linear Construction, Yokahama Museum

Public Collection

Savaria Museum Hungary

Museum of Decorative Art Montreal

Museum of Modern Art New York

Ashikaga City Museum of Art

Science Museum London

Lodz Central Museum Poland

Oita City Museum

Museum of Modern Art Gunma

Museum of Textile Art France

Public Commissions

Tokyo Budokan Tokyo, Tokyo Toritsu University, Tanabata Kaikan Fukuoka Ogohri-Shi, Ebisu Garden Place Tokyo, Act City Hamamatsu, Library of Shizu-Shi, Mandara Garden Tateyama-Shi, Foris Fuchu-Shi Tokyo, Heiwa Co. Kiryu-Shi

熊井 恭子

chika OHGI

shadows inform our understanding

空間に投影されている影で作品を理解

Chika Ohgi's works are constructed from paper that she has made herself from kozo, ganpi, cotton and ramie. The final installation is already in her mind as she makes the paper. For her the space and the work within the space take on equal value, the form and the space it will occupy becoming one integrated whole. She has written that 'the gaps between the objects and the external space (and) the outlines of the objects (are) the borders between existence and non-existence'. The particularities of the handmade paper create edges which in a peculiar way seem to form an indistinct outline creating an ambiguity between object and space. The positive/negative relationship of form in space is diffused, the cast shadows inform our understanding of the piece.

扇千花は和紙で作品を創作しています。この和紙は扇自身が楮、ガンピ、ラミー（マオ）、綿花で作成したものです。和紙を創作する際に、すでに完成作品が心の中に浮かんでいます。空間の中の作品と空間は同じくらい重要で、作品と作品が占めている空間は、1つに統合されています。物体と外部空間の境目である物体の輪郭は、存在と非存在の間の境界線でもあると扇は記しています。切れ目がはっきりとしないのが手作り和紙の特性ですが、このために物体と空間の間の輪郭を曖昧にできます。空間全体に、空間と作品の「陽と陰の関係」が見られ、空間に投影されている影で作品を理解できます。

title: Water Pillar
materials: Ganpi, Ramie & Handmade paper
size: each 5.8m high

a balance between the highly controlled and the accidental

高度な管理と偶発性の間でのバランス

Originally trained to work with print, Ohgi became interested in the nature of paper and eventually in the making of the paper itself. Her work is made up of units, within the exhibition the installation 'Walking Around The Lake' comprises 60 pieces. The installation 'Water Pillar' is also modular, the 5 towers of paper, each nearly 6 metres high, are constructed from a modular system. These pieces are free hanging allowing the work to respond to the proximity of people, to changes in humidity and movement of air. There is a balance in her work between the highly controlled and the accidental, the way in which the inadvertent gust of air reveals an unexpected aspect, providing a fresh perception of the juxtaposition of the work and the space.

The unitary method of construction is a device enabling her to cover large areas. The scale of Ohgi's installations extends the work beyond our visual periphery. Therefore rather than look 'at' the work our understanding is enhanced by our becoming 'part of' the work. This is a major intention of the artist at every stage of her conception and making. Ohgi sees the various minor changes created by the physical interaction of random elements caused by the close presence of the viewer as an essential part of the installation. The perception of the work therefore is one of a differing focus across, through and around the work, inviting speculation about visibility, invisibility, structure, weight and weightlessness.

もともとプリント作品の研鑽を受けている扇は、和紙の持つ特質に興味を惹かれ、和紙で作品を創作するようになりました。扇の作品はいくつかの小作品で構成されています。展示会の「Walking around the lake」という出展作品は60の小作品から成っています。「Water Pillar」という出展作品も、いくつかの小作品で構成している作品形式で、各々6メートルの高さの5つの和紙の塔で構成されています。これらの小作品は、人が近づいた時や、空気の湿度や動きの変化に反応して自由に揺れます。作品は高度な管理と偶発性の間でバランスをとっています。意図しない突風は予想外の様相をもたらし、作品と空間の対置に対して新鮮な視点が得られます。

作品を小単位で構成する手法を採っているために、広範囲の空間を対象にできます。扇の作品の規模は、見る者の視覚的限界を越えて広がっています。作品を「眺める」のではなく、見る者が作品の「一部」となるために、作品に対する理解が深くなるのです。この芸術家の作品では、どの着想を見ても、創作者の大きな意図が感じられます。見るものが作品に近づくと、物理的な相互作用が生まれます。その成行から発生する様々な細かな変化を、扇は見逃しません。これがこの作品の根本的な要素なのです。この作品では、作品内部や作品の周囲に視点が拡大します。そして、この作品を鑑賞する者は、視界、視界外、構造、重さ、軽さに対して、思いをめぐらせるのです。

title: Walking Around The Lake
materials: Ganpi, Kozo & Cotton
size: Installation

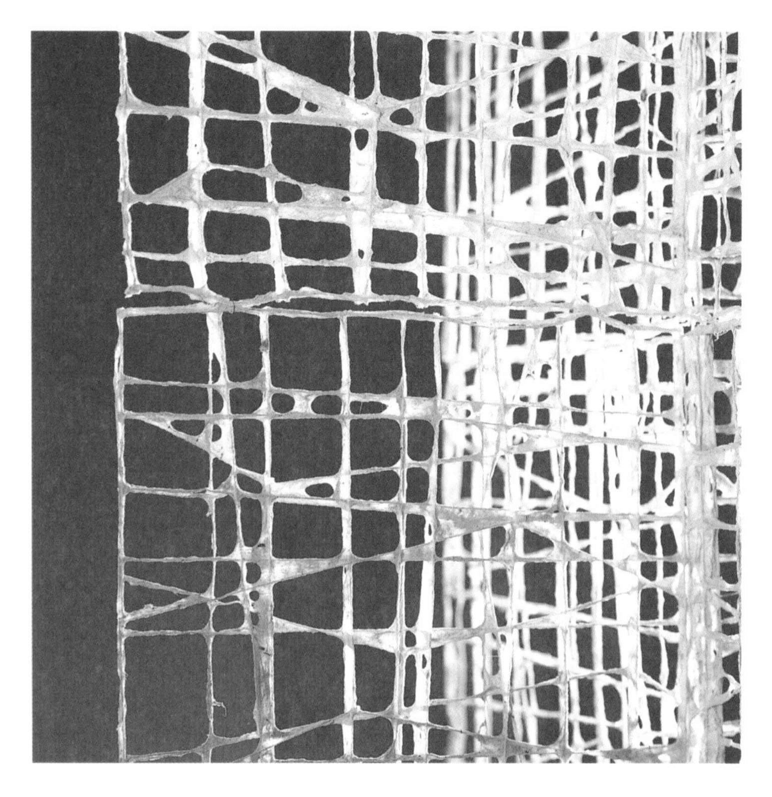

title: Water Pillar (detail)
materials: Ganpi, Ramie & Handmade paper
size: each 5.8m high

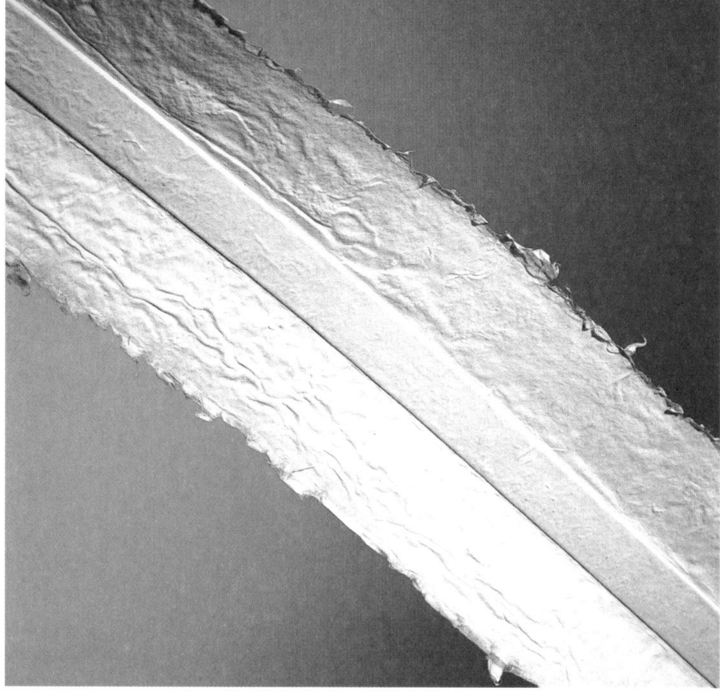

title: Walking Around The Lake (detail)
materials: Ganpi. Kozo & Cotton
size: Installation

BIOGRAPHY CHIKA OHGI

Selected Exhibitions

1981-2000	Solo Exhibitions at Gallery Gallery, Kyoto, Japan
1992	Biennale International de Lausanne, Musee Cantonal des Beaux-Arts, Lausanne Switzerland
1993	International Prize Hoppeland Art and Textile, Poperinge, Belgium
1994	Light and Shadow - Japanese Artists in Space, North Dakota Museum of Art, U.S.A.
1995	The World of Paper, National Museum of Art, Osaka, Japan
1996	Paper Art Fashion, Museum Für Kunst und Gewerbe, Hamburg, Germany
1997	The Repro-Action of Form, The Museum of Modern Art, Shiga, Japan
1998	Solo Exhibition Canberra Museum and Gallery, Australia
2000	The Memories of Algae, Rias Ark Museum of Art, Miyagi, Japan Emerging Images, Mitaka City Arts Centre, Tokyo, Japan

Awards

1994	Excellence Prize, Kyoto Crafts Biennale
1996	Grand Prix 4th International Betonac, Belgium

Public Collections

Rias Ark Museum, Miyagi, Japan

扇
千
花

Koji TAKAKI

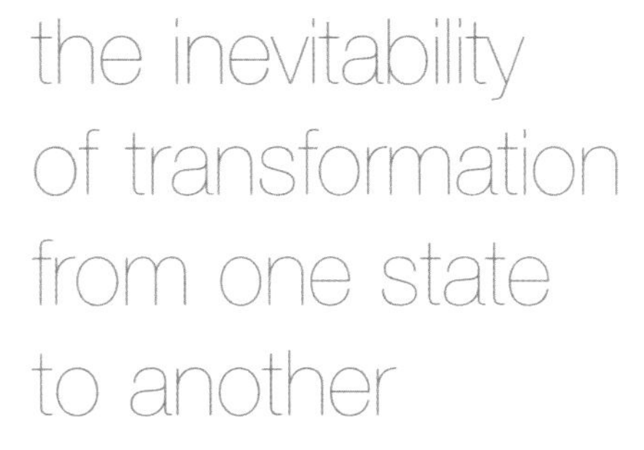

the inevitability of transformation from one state to another

変化する状態の必然性

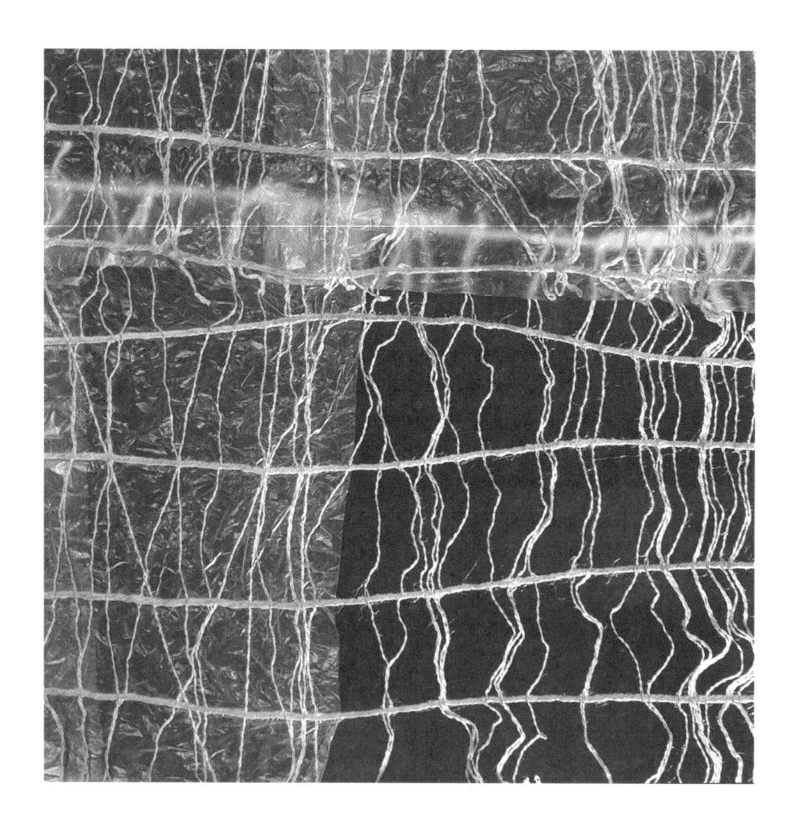

■ Initially Koji Takaki used the raw cotton cloth as the starting and finishing points of his work. Between these two points the cloth was washed at least 60 times so that the threads were exposed to reflect the erosion caused through handling. In his new work, shown in the exhibition, he is still making a reverse journey, taking the finished cloth back to its original threads, revealing the structure of the textile. The effects of the passage of time are in all Takaki's work; the disintegrating materials carry the inevitability of transformation from one state to another.

■ もともと高木光司は、作品を開始するときと仕上げるときに、木綿の布を使っていました。この開始と仕上げの間に布を少なくとも60回は洗い、糸を伸ばします、今回の新しい出展作品でも、根源へと戻る旅、完成した布を元々の糸へと還元する旅に出ています。そうすることにより、織り布の構造を明らかにするのです。高木の全作品では、時間経過の影響も効果として使っています。時間と共に素材が分解され、必然的に状態が変化していきます。

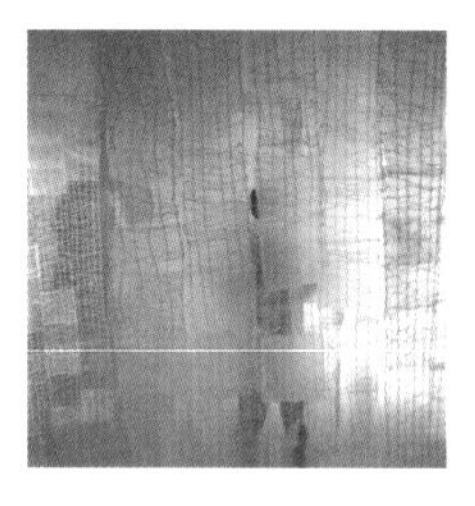

title: Ma
materials: Water-Soluble Film, Polypropylene, Linen Thread & Steel
size: Each unit 1.90m x 0.60m

a quality of membrane or skin stretched beween the sketeton of stitch

縫い目の骨格の間に、皮膚や膜があるように見えます。

Takaki's original structural starting point derived from the natural methods of drying domestic and practical cloths used in rural China. These methods have not changed in millennia and for Takaki these drying cloths are synonymous with the Chinese landscape. Cotton is a functional, non-precious material common to all classes, societies and conditions of people. It is hard wearing and bares the traces of use. Takaki's work takes the form of multiples which reflect the unspecific nature of the individual unit and re-emphasises the breadth of the universality of the material, either cotton or 'plastic'. Within this exhibition his concerns are with light and air which he explores through the use of linen thread, water-soluble film and polypropylene. The polypropylene is machine stitched in sections with linen thread onto narrow strips of water-soluble film. The strips are then washed, dissolving the water-soluble film, revealing the underpinning structure of the accumulated threads and the small polypropylene elements.

These works have a quality of membrane or skin stretched between the skeleton of stitch. Hung to move in the air sometimes in windows, against the light their transparency gives an illusion of fragility. Interestingly Takaki trained initially as a dyer and the very deliberate absence of colour in his work again reflects the passage of time, time being the natural discharger of colour.

中国の田舎で日常的に使われている布を自然に乾か
手法に基づき、高木は根本的な構造を創り始めます
これらの手法は、数千年間変化していません。高木
この手法で布を乾燥させる際に、中国の景観をも再
しているのです。木綿は、どの階層、社会、人々も
使用している実利的な安価な素材です。擦り切れに
く、頻繁な使用に耐えます。高木の作品は複数の単
で構成され、その各々の単位が一般的な本質を表現
しています。その作品は、木綿かプラスチックであ
素材の幅広い普遍性を更に強調しています。高木は
この展示作品では光と空気に関心を寄せ、これをリ
ンの糸、水溶性の薄膜、ポリプロピレンを使用しな
がら探索しています。ポリプロピレンは、水溶性の
細くて長い薄膜の上に、リネン糸で機械縫いします
次に、これを洗って水溶性の薄膜を分解すると、縫
た糸と細かなポリプロピレンの下の構造が見えて
きます。

これらの作品では、縫い目の骨格の間に、皮膚や膜
あるように見えます。窓などに吊り、空気で揺れな
ら光があたると、その透明感により繊細な幻想が浮
び上がります。興味深いことに、高木はもともと染
職人として研鑽されていますが、彼の作品では、色
が非常に慎重に取り除かれています。ここでも時の
流れが表現されています。時と共に色あせていく色
表されているのです。

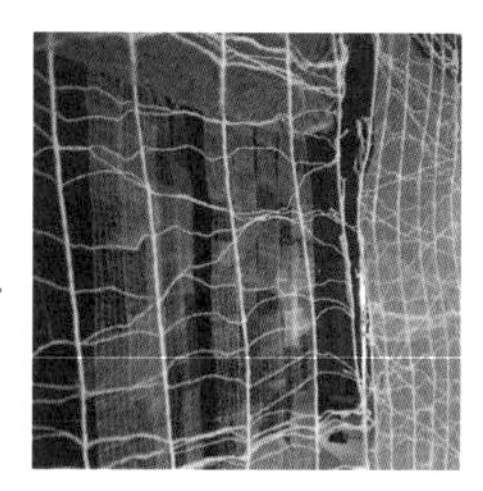

title: Ma
materials: Water-Soluble Film, Polypropylene, Linen Thread & Steel
size: each 0.7m sq. x 2.1m

title: Ma (detail)
materials: Water-Soluble Film, Polypropylene, Linen Thread & Steel
size: each 0.7m sq. x 2.1m

BIOGRAPHY KOJI TAKAKI

Selected Exhibitions

1990-99	Solo exhibitions Gallery Gallery, Kyoto, Japan
1985	Biennale International de Lausanne, Musee Cantonal des Beaux-Arts, Lausanne, Switzerland
1987	Fabric and Thread in contemporary Art, Wacoal Art Centre, Tokyo, Japan
1988	Perth International Craft Triennale, Perth, Australia
1991	Art Scene: Each Material Each Expression, The Museum of Modern Art, Tokusima, Japan
1993	Waves, Cambridge, Ontario, Canada
1994	Light and Shadow – Japanese Artists in Space, North Dakota Museum of Art, U.S.A.
1996	Ve Triennale Internationale des Mini-textiles, Musee d'Angers, France
1998	Kyo.Ma '98 - Multidisciplinary Exchange, Higasi Honganji Temple, Kyoto, Japan
1999	Kimono as Canvas, Gallery East, Freemantle, Australia

高木 光司

yoshiko TANABE

the form has the potential to expand infinitely

この作品の様式には、無限に広がる可能性があります。

■ Through her 'Endless Net Way' series Yoshiko Tanabe is pointing us towards the universality of the cellular structure. Her work also reflects a concern with invisible webs such as computer networks and the sense of their continuous spread. There is no perceivable limit to these communication webs and Tanabe's work can be seen also as having no beginning and no end and no defined centre. By this means she is asking us as viewers to continue the process of replication within our imaginations.

The 'Net Way' is created by a hyperbolic surface, which is endlessly repeated, the internal space of the structure replicating the external net structure. The brass and coloured polypropylene wire she uses are essentially malleable, the 'Net Way' being created through a knotting technique developed by Tanabe. This technique enables her to work in a confined space, using a unitary device to create large-scale works. The initial working process involves minimum energy but the form has the potential to expand infinitely, forming a parallel with cellular multiplication, exponentially increasing the energy requirement as the work grows. Tanabe sees the work as reflecting the generation of early life in a gravity-less environment; an analogy which she uses is that of life beginning in the ocean. Computer generated images of fractals and artificial life have also had an influence on the initial stages of the development of the work. Her continuing reference to cellular structures, and that these can be effected and transformed by environmental conditions, have resulted in a desire to make work that is changeable within each exhibition space.

■ 田辺由子の作品「Endless Net Way」シリーズを見る者は、粗織構造の普遍性に気づきます。また、この作品シリーズには、コンピューターネットワークなどの見えざる網（ウェブ）と、その絶えざる拡大感覚への関心も表されています。通信ネットワークには限界がなさそうに思えますが、田辺の作品にも、始まりも終わりも特定の中心もないと考えることができます。この手法により、見る者は想像の中で作品を再現し続けるのです。

この「ネットの道」は表層部分の誇張から生まれ、終わることなく続きます。作品構造の内部空間に、外部のネット構造を再現しています。真鍮と着色ポリプロピレンのワイヤは基本的に加工できるため、田辺が開発した結合技術を使用して「ネットの道」を創造します。この技術により各部分をまとめ、閉鎖空間に大規模な作品を創作できます。創作過程の第1段階では、最小限のエネルギーしか必要ありません。しかし、この作品の様式には、無限に広がる可能性があります。細胞を複製しながら創作が進み、必要なエネルギーが幾何学級的に増していきます。この作品は無重力で暮らし始めた世代を表している、そしてこの世代は海で発生した生命体に似ていると田辺は考えています。フラクタル理論によるコンピューター作成画像と人工生命体も、作品の作成第1段階に影響を与えています。細胞構造と環境条件が細胞構造に影響を与えて変化させることについて常日頃語っている田辺は、作品を展示空間ごとに変化させたいと望んでいます。

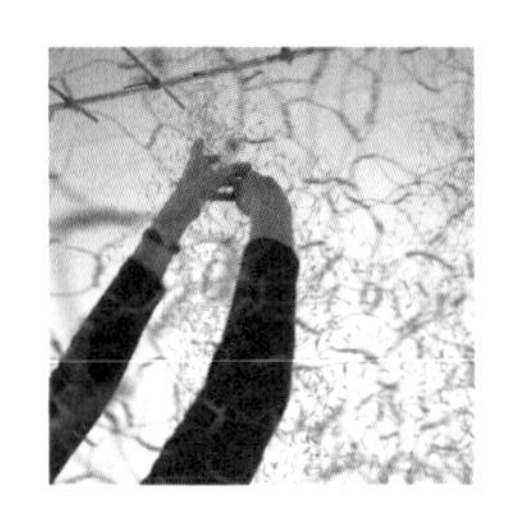

title: Endless Net Way
materials: Brass Wire
size: Installation

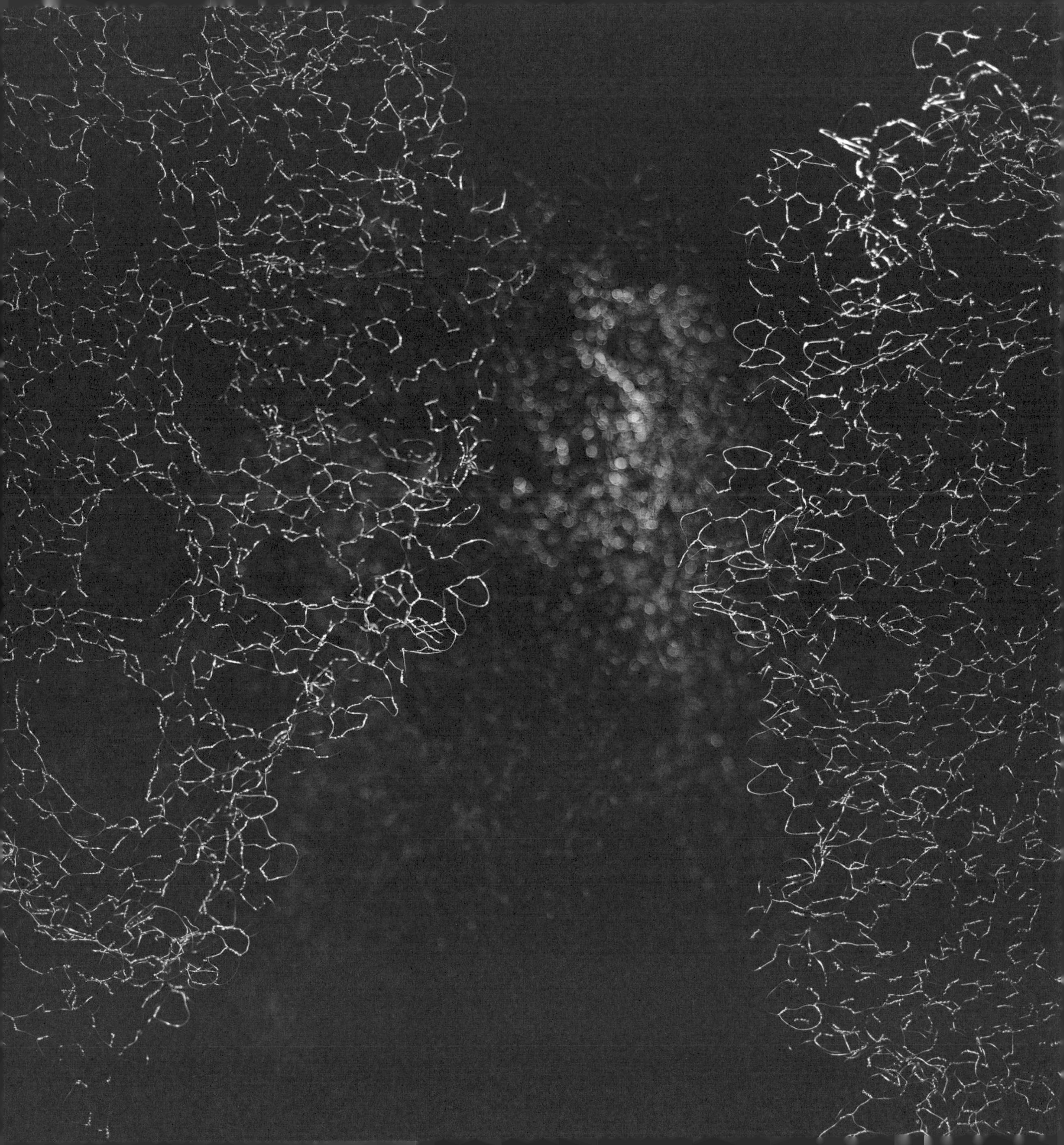

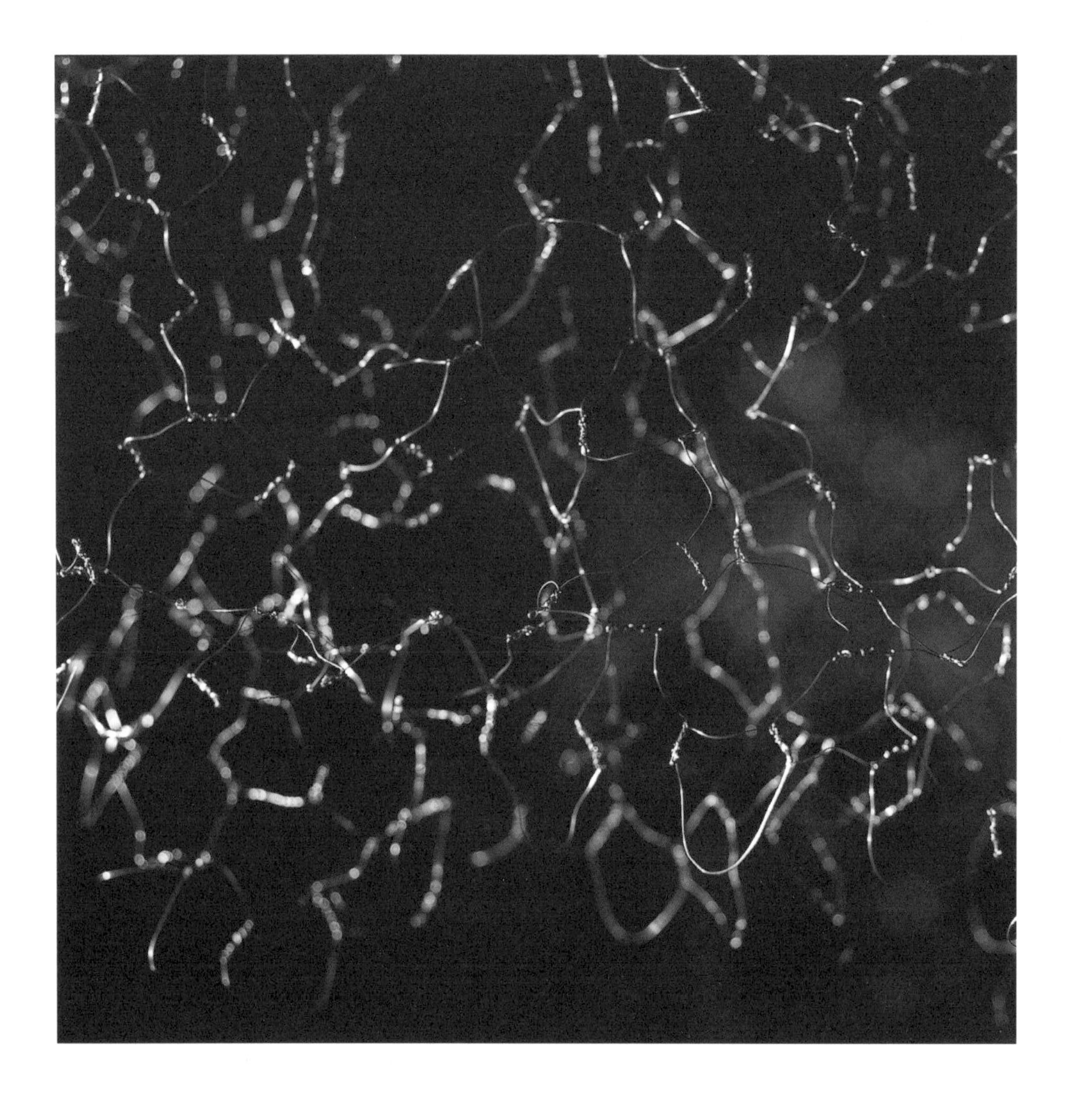

title: Endless Net Way (detail)
materials: Brass Wire
size: Installation

BIOGRAPHY YOSHIKO TANABE

Selected Exhibitions

1985 Kyoto Art Crafts, Kyoto Prefectural Centre for Arts and Culture, Japan

1990 Kyoto Selected Exhibition of Crafts Arts, Kyoto Prefectural Centre for Arts and Culture, Japan

1994 Kyoto Craft Arts Biennale, The Museum of Kyoto, Japan

1995 International Taoestry Triennale, Lodz, Poland
Contemporary Direction in Japanese Fibre Art, Kyoto Municipal Gallery, Japan

1997 The Filling of New Arts, Takashimaya Art Gallery, Tokyo/Yokohama/Osaka/Kyoto
Common Space 2, Pezinok Central Park, Slovakia

1998 Kyoto Arts Festival

1999 International Textile Competition, Museum of Kyoto, Japan

2000 Kyoto Exhibition of Art and Craft, Selected Section, Museum of Kyoto, Japan

Prizes

Grand Prix 'Creating Kyoto', Kurodani Temple, Shinnyodo Temple, Munetada Shrine, Kyoto, Japan

田辺 由子

chiyoko TANAKA

work reflects spiritual and physical relationship with surroundings

作品の表層部分は、外界に対する精神と物理的な関係を表しています。

■ Chiyoko Tanaka is a weaver who sees her work very much as part of a continuum reflecting the tradition of the woven silk textiles of Kyoto, the 1,200 year old former capital of Japan where the Nishiki woven silks originated. The process of weaving is central to her work, as she says 'the beautifully stretched warp being covered by weft threads one after another – the simple reality of the relationship between warp and weft threads as a construct…' The act of weaving is, as Tanaka says, an accumulation of weft threads, one by one, representing time passing; the resulting texture, the cloth, being the locus of the present time. In the development of the work she sets up a vertical time axis and a horizontal space axis, the weaving process is one of transforming the weft into accumulated space. The crossing points, which physically vanish as the work progresses, continue to exist as integral features of the work.

The dying process again is a direct reference to 'time'. The cone of yarn is dyed in its entirety allowing the dye to slowly permeate the yarn with the resulting graduation of colour a visual indicator of time. After weaving the cloth, it is laid on the ground and Tanaka commences the process she describes as 'Grinding'. This process is to trace the ground texture as well as 'Grinding' out the surface texture. An additional effect is achieved by the application of certain soils as in 'Ochre No. 300', charcoal as in 'Permeated Black 1 & 2', or in the use of particular tools in 'Blue Threads & Sienna' where brick from Sienna was used, in 'Blue Threads & Grey' where white stone was used.

■ 田中千世子は自らを、現代に営々と受け継がれている京都の絹織物伝統の一環である織り職人と考えています。京都は1200年の伝統を持つ日本の古都であり、絹織物の錦織りが生まれたところです。田中の作品の中心は、織るという工程です。「美しく縫った経糸を緯糸で1つ1つ覆い、経糸と緯糸の関連性をシンプルに具現した構成主義の作品」と田中は表現しています。田中によると、縫うという行為は、1つ1つの緯糸の積み重ねです。時の経過を表し、織り地や布に現時点での時間を表現しています。作品を創作する際、垂直に時間軸を、水平に空間軸を取ります。縫いながら、緯糸を構築空間へと変革していきます。創作が進むにつれて糸の交差は消滅し、統合された1つの作品として存在するようになります。

染めるという作業過程も、「時間」を直接的に表しています。染料がゆっくりと糸に染み入るように糸を染めます。その結果、色彩にグラデュエーションが生まれ、時間の経過を目で見られます。縫った後に布を床に置き、田中は「研磨」と呼んでいる工程を開始します。この工程では表面の織地を「研磨」するだけでなく、研磨した織物に模様を施していきます。「Ochre No.300」では土を、「Permeated Black 1&2」では木炭を加え、「Blue Threads & Sienna」では独自の道具によりシエナの煉瓦を、「Blue Threads & Grey」では白い石を、それぞれ使用して更なる効果を醸し出しています。「Ochre No.200」に使用した土は、京都の聚楽第で見つけたものです。これは家庭や茶室の内装に伝統的に使われているものです。「Permeated Black 1&2」では、織物の裏側を石炭で擦っています。表側の表層部分を地面の小さな石で浮き彫りにし、石炭の粉を裏側から表側へと通しています。

title: Ochre No. 300
materials: Raw Linen & Jarakudai Soil
size: 0.94m x 5.23m

conscious reference to the importance of the six senses within buddhism

The soil used for 'Ochre No. 200' is found in the Jurakadai area of Kyoto and was traditionally used as interior wall surfaces in homes and teahouses. With 'Permeated Black 1 & 2' the reverse side of these fabrics was rubbed using a stone with charcoal. The surface of the front side became embossed by the tiny stones on the ground and the charcoal powder was forced through from the reverse side to the front.

The surface of the work reflects Tanaka's spiritual and physical relationship with her surroundings, and in the same way all the structural elements in her work also carry symbolic significance. In the diptych 'Permeated Black 1 & 2' both works are divided into six sections, 'Blue Threads and Sienna' and 'Blue Threads & Grey' each are divided into three sections making six in total. This is a conscious reference to the importance of the six senses or 'ways' within Buddhism. In some works, including the 'Blue Threads' pieces, the centre section is left unwoven with the weft from one side carried across in a diagonal line representing the 'vanishing point'. The warp ends of each work are cut in a particular way and left exposed as a reminder of the vertical and the horizontal, the warp and the weft, time and space.

作品の表層部分は、田中の外界に対する精神と物理的な関係を表しています。同様に、作品の構成要素すべてに象徴的な意味があります。「Permeated Black 1 & 2」のディプティクでは、双方の作品を6セクションに分けています。「'Blue Threads from Sienna' and 'Blue Threads & Grey'」では各々を3セクションに分け、合わせて6セクションにしています。この作品は、仏教の「しきたり」や第6感の重要性を知覚に訴えています。すなわち、「Blue Threads」などの作品の中心的なセクションは、緯糸で斜め模様に縫っていない左側の部分であり、「消失点」を表しています。各作品における経糸の終点は、独特の手法で切っています。切った糸をそのまま見えるように残し、垂直、水平、経糸、緯糸、時間、空間を思い出させるのです。

1

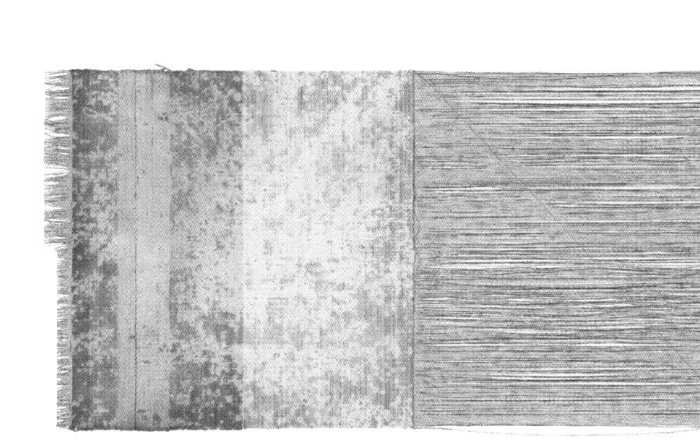

2

3

仏教の「しきたり」や第6感の重要性を知覚に訴えています。

title: Blue Threads And Grey [2]
materials: Raw Linen, Ramie, Silk, Cotton & White Stone
size: 0.315m x 0.975m

title: Blue Threads And Sienna [3]
materials: Linen, Ramie & Brick From Sienna
size: 0.315m x 0.96m

title: Permeated Black 1 & 2 [1]
materials: Silk, Ramie, Linen & Charcoal
size: Each 2.34m x 0.38m

title: Ochre No. 300 (detail)
materials: Raw Linen & Jarakudai Soil
size: 0.94m x 5.23m

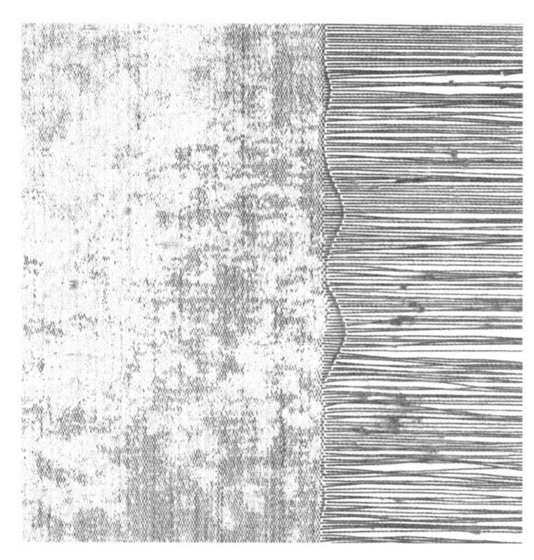

title: Blue Threads And Sienna (detail)
materials: Linen, Ramie & Brick From Sienna
size: 0.315m x 0.96m

title: Blue Threads And Grey (detail)
materials: Raw Linen, Ramie, Silk, Cotton & White Stone
size: 0.315m x 0.975m

title: Permeated Black 1 & 2 (detail)
materials: Silk, Ramie, Linen &Charcoal
size: Each 2.34m x 0.38m

BIOGRAPHY CHIYOKO TANAKA

Selected Exhibitions

1987	Expression/Construction of Filament, Wacoal Art Centre, Tokyo, Japan
1988	Art Now, Hyogo Prefectural Museum of Modern Art, Kobe, Japan
1992-3	Kohyama and Tanaka: Contemporary Ceramics and Textiles from Japan Museum het Princessehof, Leeuwarden, Holland/Museum of Arts and Crafts, Hamburg, Germany/The Museum of Modern Art, Shiga, Japan
1993	Applied Art Collected By Benno Premsela, Stedelijk Museum, Amsterdam, Holland
1993-4	Focus on Fibre Art – Selection from the Growing 20th Century Collection, The Art Institute of Chicago, U.S.A.
1993-5	Waves – Contemporary Japanese Fibreworks, Touring Canada
1996	Cinque Magiciens Textile du Japon, Passage de Retz, Paris, France
1996-7	Textile Wizards From Japan, The Isreael Museum, Jerusalem, Israel
1998-0	Structure and Surface: Contemporary Japanese Textiles, Museum of Modern Art, New York and Touring U.S.A.

Prizes

1997	Bronze Prize, 6th International Tapestry Triennale, Lodz, Poland

Collections

Museum of Arts and Crafts, Hamburg, Germany, The Art Institute of Chicago, U.S.A., The St. Louis Museum, U.S.A., Stedelijk Museum, Amsterdam, Holland, The Pulitzer Collection, St. Louis, U.S.A., The Israel Museum, Jerusalem, Israel, Passage de Retz, Paris, France

田中 千世子